THE TREE COUNCIL

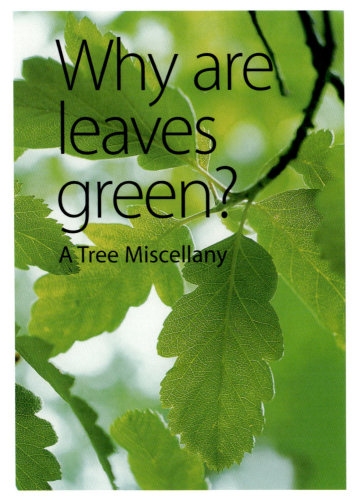

Why are leaves green?

A Tree Miscellany

Jon Stokes and John White
Photography: Archie Miles

Foreword

The trees of our gardens, streets, parks, fields, hedges, hillsides, forests and woodlands enrich our lives in countless ways. They are often, however, so much a part of our surroundings and our daily lives that we subconsciously assume we know them well. Yet hidden in their roots, their bark, their leaves, their flowers and fruits are many marvels to be discovered and puzzles to be solved.

What is a tree made of? How deep do roots go? How much water does a tree use? How many leaves are on that apple tree? Why do leaves change colour in the autumn? Which is the world's oldest tree? Which is the biggest tree in Britain? And which is the smallest?

These questions, and many many more, are what "Why are leaves green? – A Tree Miscellany" is all about. In an ever changing world, the constantly expanding scope of knowledge can often provide the key to new or different answers to age-old questions. Although the answers are from tree professionals, even they will readily admit they are not always infallible and that there are many questions about trees to which definitive answers have yet to be found.

This book will certainly answer at least some of the questions that you would like to ask. However, we hope that it will also encourage you to look at trees through rather different eyes. Prepare to be intrigued, surprised and occasionally amazed by the hidden secrets they hold.

Pauline Buchanan Black

Introduction

The inspiration for this book came from two groups of Tree Wardens – in South Somerset and West Sussex – keen to have answers to some of the questions about trees that they were frequently being asked. So The Tree Council decided to help.

We asked all the volunteers in our national Tree Warden Scheme, as well as a number of local authority tree officers, what questions they most often faced – and received over 5,000 questions in reply. The ones included in this book are those that cropped up most often. This publication therefore covers a very diverse range of topics about trees.

We have grouped questions in chapters and sections and there is also an index to help find answers on related topics.

No book of this type can be exhaustive, and we are sure there are many other questions that we could have tackled. However we hope that this book will answer many of the queries people have about trees.

The Tree Council

Environmental charity The Tree Council is a partnership of organisations working together for more trees, of the right kind, in the right places; for better care for all trees, of all ages; and to inspire effective action for trees. Its goal is to make trees matter to everyone.

It was founded in 1974, with government backing, as the umbrella body for UK organisations involved in tree planting, care and conservation. The idea was to keep up the momentum of National Tree Planting Year 1973 (with its slogan of "Plant a Tree in '73"). Today the Tree Council's members range from professional, non-governmental, specialist and trade organisations, including other conservation charities, to local authorities and government bodies.

One of The Tree Council's first actions (in 1975) was to organise National Tree Week, and this winter planting festival has become the UK's largest annual celebration of trees and woods. More recently we have introduced other annual initiatives – the Tree Care Campaign (March to September), Walk in the Woods (throughout May), and Seed Gathering Season (mid September to mid October) – all, like National Tree Week, aimed at involving as many people as possible in planting, caring for and enjoying trees and woods.

We also work with our member organisations on particular issues of concern. We are, for example, leading the Green Monuments Campaign – a major drive for proper safeguards for heritage trees – and the Hedge Tree Campaign in support of the Government Biodiversity Action Plan.

Fundamental to much of this is The Tree Council's Tree Warden Scheme, run in partnership with National Grid and the Department for Communities and Local Government. Tree Wardens form a national force of volunteers, in local networks, dedicated to their communities' trees.

They are appointed by parish councils, local authorities and community groups to help protect trees in their own neighbourhoods and to increase their numbers. They work closely with professionals, such as tree officers, who are often key to the success of the scheme.

Typical Tree Warden activities include protecting trees, growing, planting and caring for new ones, gathering information about local trees and developing imaginative projects with schools. See page 100 for more about Tree Wardening.

For further information visit
www.treecouncil.org.uk

National Grid

National Grid is an international energy delivery business and is the UK's largest investor-owned utility and one of the largest worldwide utility companies.

The company owns and operates the high voltage electricity transmission system in England and Wales which provides electricity to the local distribution companies, who in turn provide electricity to homes and businesses. In addition National Grid owns and operates the gas transmission system in Great Britain which provides gas to the local distribution networks, four of which are also owned by National Grid. The company operates and maintains the infrastructure of overhead lines, underground cables and gas pipelines 24 hours a day, 365 days a year to ensure that the nation's energy requirement is delivered safely, reliably and efficiently.

National Grid is committed to the protection and enhancement of the environment, always seeking new ways to minimise the environmental impacts of its past, present and future activities. Believing that everyone is responsible for good environmental performance, the company incorporates environmental considerations into all its business activities.

National Grid has worked in partnership with The Tree Council since 1990 and has supported its national Tree Warden Scheme since 1997. The expert advice National Grid receives from The Tree Council, together with the support of Tree Wardens, is vital in helping the company to manage trees in a safe and sustainable way.

For more information about National Grid visit **www.nationalgrid.com**

Communities and Local Government

Communities and Local Government is backing The Tree Council's Tree Warden Scheme with funding from the special grants programme in support of the Government's wider 'Cleaner, Safer, Greener' initiative . This is tackling important issues about the places where people live, work and play.

The quality of our local environment affects the quality of all our lives – we use public spaces on a daily basis and are affected by their condition. Successful, thriving and prosperous communities are characterised by streets, parks and open spaces that are safe, clean and attractive – 'liveable' places, that local people are proud of.

The Government is responsible for developing policy to enhance the 'liveability' of public spaces, whilst local authorities are responsible for delivering improvements on the ground. Responsibility for public spaces is shared, and many organisations and individuals, including local authorities, voluntary groups and members of the public directly influence their quality.

The grant The Tree Council receives from Communities and Local Government is helping to deliver 'liveability' by enabling The Tree Council to extend Tree Wardening further into towns and cities.

For more information about Communities and Local Government visit **www.communities.gov.uk**

For information about the Government's 'Cleaner, Safer, Greener' initiative see **www.cleanersafergreener.gov.uk**

Contents

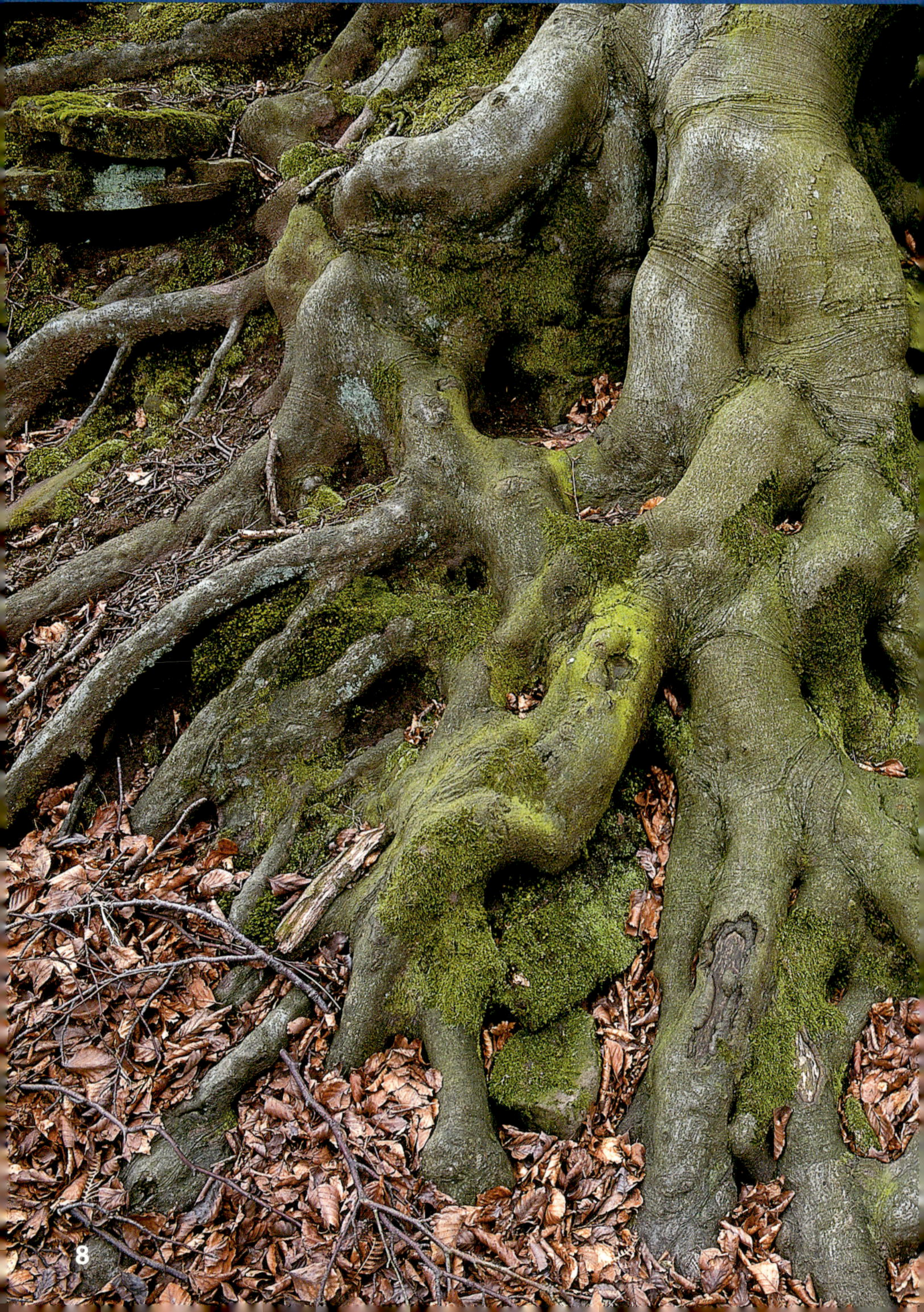

What is a tree?

In this book we have used the definition that 'a tree is regarded as a plant that has a self-supporting perennial woody stem', which covers everything from a tiny dwarf willow to a towering giant redwood, and we don't worry about the distinction between shrubs and trees.

Although this appears to be a simple question, in fact it is quite complicated. Simplistically, a tree is a 'large' woody organism. That definition, however, is inadequate, for example, in the case of small willows which are 'small' woody organisms, yet can be described as 'trees'. Another definition is that a tree is any plant that has a self-supporting perennial (i.e. living more than one year) woody stem. This definition works better than the previous one, except when considering the distinction between a tree and a shrub.

Some tree books have created the distinction that a tree has a single trunk and an elevated head of branches, whereas a shrub branches from the base, with no obvious trunk. Unfortunately, the way 'a tree' is managed can thus make it 'a shrub'; or 'a shrub' that has not been cut can become 'a tree'.

Interestingly, in the Tree Preservation Order (TPO) legislation (see page 98) the term 'tree' is not defined in the Act, nor does the Act limit the application of TPOs to trees of a minimum size. Indeed for the purposes of the TPO legislation, the High Court has held that a 'tree' is "anything which ordinarily one would call a tree."

Ancient willow growing in adverse conditions in Newfoundland. Little more than 30 cm (1 foot) across, this tree is estimated to be 150 years old.

How many tree species are native to the UK?

This is another difficult question. The term 'native tree' is based on those trees that colonized the British Isles naturally after the last Ice Age (c10,000 years ago) and before these islands were cut off from the rest of Europe by the rising sea levels. The following 33 species (see list A) are the usually quoted native trees.

Curiously, however, usually omitted from this list are Plymouth pear and wild pear which would bring the total to 35. Then there are 16 other species of rare and endemic (found only in the UK) whitebeams (see list B) which are seldom counted but which would take the total to 51.

The true service tree (*Sorbus domestica*) – which is probably a native based on an isolated colony found growing on the cliffs of South Wales – would make 52.

In addition there are the willows (which most people regard as shrubs but for the purposes of this book are trees – list C) which would take the total to 66. Other plants which are usually thought of as shrubs, but we call trees for the purpose of this book, would take the total to 76 (list D).

Finally there are a few trees and shrubs whose origins are confused: such as barberry, English elm, sycamore and white elm.

List A:
alder, ash, aspen, bay willow, beech, bird cherry, black poplar, box, common oak, crab apple, crack willow, downy birch, field maple, goat willow, hawthorn, hazel, holly, hornbeam, juniper, large-leaved lime, midland hawthorn, rowan, Scots pine, sessile oak, silver birch, small-leaved lime, strawberry tree, whitebeam, white willow, wild cherry, wild service tree, wych elm and yew

List B:
Sorbus anglica, Sorbus arranensis, Sorbus bristoliensis, Sorbus devoniensis, Sorbus eminens, Sorbus hibernica, Sorbus lancastriensis, Sorbus leptophylla, Sorbus leyana, Sorbus minima, Sorbus porrigentiformis, Sorbus pseudofennica, Sorbus rupicolu, Sorbus subcuneata, Sorbus vexans, Sorbus wilmottiana.

List C:
almond willow, common sallow, creeping willow, dark-leaved willow, downy willow, dwarf willow, eared willow, mountain willow, net-leaved willow, osier, purple willow, tea-leaved willow, whortle-leaved willow, woolly willow

List D:
alder buckthorn, blackthorn, dogwood, dwarf birch, elder, guelder rose, purging buckthorn, sea buckthorn, spindle and wayfaring tree

Tree types

How many tree species are there in the world?

It is thought that there are between 80,000 and 100,000 tree species in the world, the difference being a reflection of the difficulty of defining a 'tree' (see page 10). Of the world's tree flora, nearly nine per cent (7,388 species) are documented as being globally threatened with extinction, while over 90 tree species have already become extinct.

What is a broadleaf?

The broadleaf trees are angiosperms – plants with their seeds hidden inside a fruit. Angiosperm trees can be of two types: one produces two leaves (or more) from the seeds (dicotyledons) – e.g. oaks and birches; the other produces a single leaf from the seed (monocotyledons) – e.g. palms, aloes and yuccas. Most of the world's trees are broadleaf.

What is a conifer?

Conifers are usually thought of as trees that bear cones. However, they are actually gymnosperms – plants that have 'naked' seeds that can be seen in the cone or the fruit without having to cut it open. There are approximately 650 species of conifer around the world, which include yew and juniper. There are also many hundreds of subspecies and varieties in cultivation.

What is the difference between an evergreen and a deciduous tree?

An evergreen tree is a plant that retains green leaves all year round. A deciduous tree loses its leaves completely for part of the year, becoming bare and leafless. The terms 'evergreen' and 'deciduous' are sometimes taken as shorthand for conifers (evergreen) and broadleaves (deciduous). However, this does not work in every case as there are deciduous conifers, for example dawn redwood (*Metasequoia glyptostroboides*) and larch (*Larix decidua*), and evergreen broadleaf trees including holly (*Ilex aquifolium*).

Above: A classic spreading broadleaf tree – an open grown wych elm. Opposite (top): The distinctive form of the weeping willow. (bottom): Conifers are well adapted for snowy conditions.

Why are trees of different shapes?

Although each tree species tends to have a characteristic shape, the actual form of an individual tree develops in response to environmental forces such as wind, drought and soil type. An individual tree growing where nothing is competing with it for light, tends to develop the characteristic shape of the species. This form has been utilized for millennia to maximize fruit production (e.g. in olive groves and orchards). However, competition for light (e.g. in a woodland) will cause the tree to develop a taller form.

What is a variety?

In cultivation odd shaped trees have been artificially selected. A variety is a natural occurrence, differing from the 'normal' tree in one or more characteristics (e.g. leaf shape, colour or tree shape). Some are so successful that they almost seem to be part of the landscape (e.g. Lombardy poplar, weeping willow and Irish yew). Weeping cultivars of numerous species have been produced. Some remain constant (e.g. weeping beech) but others tend to revert to normal growth after a few years and require constant pruning. Some weeping trees are quite grotesque, particularly if a naturally tall or gigantic species is made to grovel close to the ground.

13

Wood

What is wood?

'Wood' is formed as a result of the growth of a tree. It is a hard, fibrous, substance which occurs under the tree's bark (see page 36). As a tree grows, its stem is formed of five main layers (see diagram). The inner two layers are the wood – the inner heartwood and the outer sapwood. Sapwood conducts water around the tree. Heartwood (where it is present, for it is not found in all trees) is the material usually sought for timber.

What are tree rings?

Trees grow outwards by the addition of new wood immediately under the bark. As the tree grows, it creates visible growth rings which in some species have a light and dark band within them. The differences in the widths of the rings are due to changes in growth rate from year to year. The rings can be counted to determine the age of the tree, and used to date wood taken from trees in the past: this practice is known as dendrochronology.

What is the difference between hardwood and softwood?

In spring when broadleaved trees expand their foliage, they need a faster flow of sap than conifers. The broadleaves have therefore developed special conducting channels called vessels, which give the hardwood its strength.

What is a softwood?

Hardwood and softwood are terms that were developed by the timber industry. 'Softwood' was coined to describe the wood from conifers (e.g. spruce, pine, cedar and fir). This wood is generally softer than hardwoods, but there are exceptions. For example yew, a coniferous wood, is much harder than some 'hardwoods' (e.g. poplar and lime).

What is a hardwood?

The term 'hardwood' is used to describe the wood of broadleaved trees, although some broadleaf timber (e.g. balsa) is much softer than the 'softwoods'.

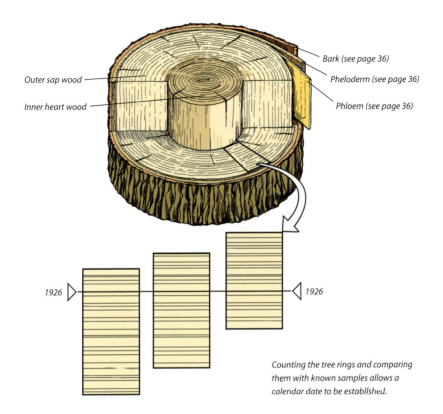

Bark (see page 36)

Pheloderm (see page 36)

Phloem (see page 36)

Outer sap wood

Inner heart wood

1926

1926

Counting the tree rings and comparing them with known samples allows a calendar date to be established.

How does dendrochronology work?

Each year trees put on a layer of new wood under the bark. Various factors influence the thickness of each annual ring – particularly weather. In favourable growing conditions the rings are wide, whilst poor growing conditions produce narrow rings. All trees growing at the same time will show a similar pattern of rings – thick, thin, thick, etc (rather like a bar-code). To use the tree ring information, ring patterns called tree-ring chronologies have been constructed. A continuous master sequence for England exists going back to about 5,000 BC. To establish the age of a piece of wood, the rings are counted and then compared to a tree-ring chronology, enabling a calendar date to be given to each ring, and the age of the timber to be established.

Which tree produces the best firewood?

As a rule of thumb all dry wood will burn, although some will spit. Green woods, except ash and holly, are more difficult to burn, because of their high water content. The calorific value of good firewood is about half that of coal. Individual qualities of firewood are described in this excerpt from an old rhyme.

Above: a massive log pile is vital for survival for the people of Raleigh in Newfoundland, both for home heating and cooking.

Below: This family group re-enacting Tudor times illustrates how important good firewood has always been for day-to-day living.

Opposite: A mature ash tree in Borrowdale, Cumbria. Ash is the best firewood, whether green or seasoned.

*Beechwood fires burn bright and clear,
Hornbeam blazes too,
If the logs are kept a year
To season through and through*

*Oak logs will warm you well
If they're old and dry
Larch logs of pinewood smell,
But the sparks will fly*

*Pine is good, and so is yew
For warmth through wintry days,
But poplar and willow too
Take long to dry or blaze*

*Birch logs will burn too fast,
Alder scarce at all,
Chestnut logs are good to last
If cut in the fall*

*Holly logs will burn like wax
You should burn them green
Elm logs like smouldering flax,
No flame is seen*

*Pear logs and apple logs
They will scent your room,
Cherry logs across the dogs
Smell like flowers in bloom*

*But ash logs, all smooth and grey,
Burn them green or old,
Buy up all that come your way,
They're worth their weight in gold.*

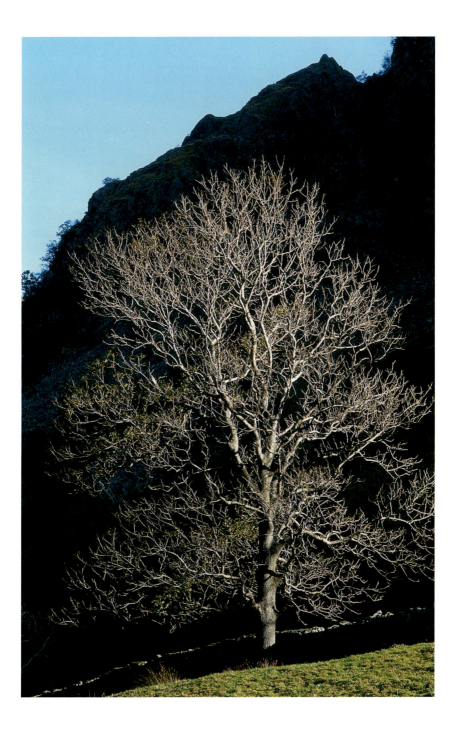

Leaves

What are leaves for?

Leaves are the elements of the plant specially designed for photosynthesis. Leaf cells contain discrete structures called chloroplasts which convert the energy of sunlight into chemical energy to produce sugars. The full photosynthetic reactions are complex but they are usually simplified as:

Carbon dioxide + Water + Light energy
(in the presence of Chlorophyll)
= Glucose (sugar) + Oxygen + Water

The plant takes in carbon dioxide to produce sugars for itself and, as a waste product, emits oxygen into the atmosphere.

How many leaves does a tree have?

A mature English oak (*Quercus robur*) has approximately 700,000 leaves whilst an American elm (*Ulmus americana*) has as many as 5,000,000 leaves. Conversely, a large apple tree may have only about 50,000.

How much oxygen can a tree produce?

This depends on the size and species of tree, but the large number of leaves on some trees allows them to produce considerable quantities of oxygen, one large beech tree producing in a year sufficient oxygen for 10 people.

Unlike deciduous trees, evergreen trees can produce some oxygen all year round.

Why do some trees have needle leaves?

Conifers have needles, instead of broad leaves, to help them to survive in areas of water stress and extreme temperature. Needle leaves enable the tree to reduce evaporation, allowing the tree to save water.

How do purple-leaved trees survive without green leaves?

Trees such as copper beech appear to be 'purple' but the green pigment is masked by increased levels of other plant pigments. In fact the leaves are green under the surface pigment and so produce food by photosynthesis in the same way as 'green' leaves. Observe copper beech leaves growing in deep shade and you will see the green showing through. This is also true of variegated, golden and other coloured varieties.

Why are leaves green?

Leaves are normally green in colour, as a result of chlorophyll from which the tree produces its food. This amazing compound uses the red and blue light in sunlight to produce the chemical reactions needed to turn carbon dioxide and water into sugars and oxygen, resulting in the green light being reflected and giving the leaf its colour.

Why do leaves change colour in the autumn?

As autumn approaches the trees reabsorb the chlorophyll from their leaves and various other pigments (carotenoids and anthocyanins) previously masked by the chlorophyll are revealed. As the leaves die, these red anthocyanins are produced in great quantity from sugars that remain in the leaf. However, this process requires warmth and bright light during the day and cold at night to reduce the chances of the sugars being withdrawn back to the tree. Therefore the nature of the autumn weather dictates the quality of the autumn colours. Ideal weather conditions are frequently found on the east coast of the USA, which results in amazing autumn leaf displays there, but less frequently in the UK.

Why do leaves fall off in the autumn?

Simply to save the tree from storm damage by reducing its resistance to wind, ice and snow. Shedding leaves also reduces water loss at a time when replacement soil moisture is limited by low temperature.

How do leaves fall off in the autumn?

With deciduous trees, the mechanism to shed leaves is called abscission. Leaf fall is not a random process, but is a deliberate sequence, triggered by decreasing daylight and reduced air temperature. Across the base of the leaf is the abscission zone which breaks as the autumn approaches, allowing the leaf to fall from the tree. The breaking of this zone is caused by increased levels of the plant hormones ethylene, abscissic acid and/or auxin. A leaf scar remains on the twig at the site of the shed leaf.

Although leaves grow to a finite size in one season, the twigs they grow on continue to expand into branches year on year so in due course all leaves, even needles, are forced to drop off.

When leaves fall off my tree what should I do with them?

When a deciduous tree drops its leaves it returns nutrients back to the ground. This is in a raw and unusable state until it is broken down by fungi and micro-organisms. Therefore where possible it is best to leave the leaves where they fall or compost the leaves so that future plant life will benefit and the nutrient cycle will be maintained. Soil moisture retention will be enhanced by the addition of organic material, and will also benefit worms.

If leaves are burned most of the nutrients are lost in the smoke. The bonfire if it is near a tree or other plant, will not only scorch the tree's branches but invariably damage or destroy any roots and kill the micro-organisms in the soil under the fire site.

Which leaves make the best compost?

All leaves will make compost but leaves on their own will tend to form a tough flat mat which takes a long time to break down. Leaves should always be mixed with other bulky vegetation such as grass. The best are probably those that decompose quickly, such as lime, sycamore or birch. Some leaves are rich in tannins, especially oak: this is why oak leaves should be well mixed with other species. Conifer needles are of limited nutritional value but their stiffness will add structure and air-spaces to the finished compost. Hard evergreens such as holly are difficult to manage but will eventually rot down. A small number of trees (e.g. laurel, rhododendron and yew) are toxic and should preferably be left out of the compost heap altogether.

Why are there different shapes of tree leaves?

Leaf shape depends on cell division that is controlled by the genetic make up of the tree. The objective of a leaf is to capture light from the sun to manufacture plant food. The specific kind of leaf depends on what is best for the particular plant in its natural habitat. In trees large simple leaves tend to shade each other out. A modification adopted by some trees with simple leaves is asymmetry; often the leaf base will be oblique or the blade lop-sided. The result of asymmetry is that the slightest breeze will move leaves in and out of sun and shade.

Another modification of the simple leaf is the palmate (maple-like) type often with a long 'drip-tip' on the lobes and occasionally a cordate (heart-shaped) base. All these triangular points tend to mesh with one another to capture available light. Some palmate leaves may be reduced to a consistent number of leaflets (e.g. bifoliate or trifoliate).

A compound leaf (e.g. horse chestnut) takes this splitting of a single leaf a stage further. The deep shade under a horse chestnut tree is testament to how efficient this kind of divided leaf is at intercepting light. If the leaflets on a compound leaf are variable in size, number and arrangement, the leaf may be described as pinnate (e.g. ash or walnut).

Top right: compound leaf (horse chestnut)
Top left: pinnate leaf (ash)
Centre: simple leaf (wych elm)
Bottom: palmate leaf (Japanese maple).

How do evergreen trees renew their leaves?

Evergreen trees renew their leaves in much the same way as deciduous trees, but less obviously. The leaf stalk is often fairly rigid and the abscission joint is swollen, so the leaf is only forced to fall by the increase in girth of the stem bearing it. Most old evergreen leaves fall in spring as new leaves develop. The leaves of some trees remain firmly fixed for around three years (e.g. holly); others shed most leaves one year after they were produced (e.g. Mirbeck oak).

Flowers

Why do only a few trees produce blossom?

Every tree has a flower but many of them are not readily visible. Trees are generally pollinated in three ways – by animals, by insects and by the wind. If the tree has to attract animals or insects, the flowers need to attract the pollinators by means of bright colours, smells or nectar. The flowers of these trees are usually referred to as blossom. However, if the tree is wind pollinated it has no need for bright petals, scent or nectar and in consequence trees like elm and oak produce small inconspicuous flowers that may not be noticed.

Can trees cause hay fever?

All trees produce pollen and some trees can cause hay fever in some hay fever sufferers. The most important pollen type for hay fever sufferers in the UK is grass pollen, but during the early part of the year tree pollen can affect a small percentage of people. Some tree pollen – (e.g. alder and hazel) can be about in January and February, followed by yew, most conifers, elm, willow and ash in March. Next is silver birch which affects 25 percent of hay fever sufferers during April. In late April to mid May oak tree pollen is about, although oak affects fewer sufferers than birch.

Why does my ash tree appear to change sex?

Ash trees (*Fraxinus excelsior* L.), have flowers which may be male, female, or hermaphrodite. The flowers open before the leaves, and while both male and female flowers can occur on the same tree, it is common to find all male and all female trees. Surprisingly, however, a tree that is all male one year can produce female flowers the next, and similarly a female tree can become male. How this happens, or the mechanism that controls these changes is still unknown.

Ash flowers.

Wind pollinated flowers of hornbeam (above) and insect pollinated flowers of horse chestnut (right).

Why do trees have flowers?

Flowering plants are known as angiosperms and are dominant on earth today. The purpose of the flower is to produce seed for reproduction. They appeared in the Cretaceous period some 120 million years ago by gradually adapting from spore-bearing plants that preceded them. Morphologically a flower is a modified spore-bearing shoot. The purpose of a flower is reproduction by the production of seed. In order to maintain genetic diversity it is important that individuals interact with others and not themselves. Flowers have many intricate designs and shapes, often co-operating with the animal kingdom, especially insects, to prevent self-fertilization.

Fruit AND Seed

Why don't my holly and yew have berries?

Some trees have flowers of both sexes on one tree (monoecious trees) which means that each tree can produce fruit. Other trees have flowers of only one sex (dioecious trees). For dioecious trees, like yew and holly, to produce berries, it is necessary to have a female tree with a male tree within pollinating distance. When the flowers of a female tree are fertilized they will produce berries.

Are yew berries poisonous?

Yes, the centre of a yew fruit – the seed – is poisonous. However, the red fleshy part around the seed – the aril – is actually the only part of a yew tree that is not poisonous.

Why is a lime tree so called when it doesn't grow limes?

The British lime tree appears to take its name from the Germanic root *lind*, which became *linde* or *linne* in Anglo Saxon, suggesting 'flexible' with reference to the tree's wood and inner bark. Neither the name nor the tree is in any way related to the citrus fruit called 'lime' (*Citrus aurantiifolia*). Carl Linnaeus, the 18th century Swedish naturalist developed the binomial naming

system giving each species a genera name (e.g. *Citrus*) and a species name (e.g. *aurantiifolia*) exactly to avoid this sort of confusion.

The bright pink berries of yew. The seed inside is poisonous, but the pink aril is not.

Are acorns poisonous?

Green acorns are poisonous to ponies. In the New Forest, Hampshire, and in other forests (see page 50) there exists the right of pannage. This is a legal right for 'Commoners' (people with special rights in the Forest) to turn out domestic pigs (which love green acorns) into a wood or forest, in order that they may feed on fallen acorns and remove them before the ponies eat them. Although acorns are not poisonous to humans, eating them is not recommended.

Seeds from apples rarely grow true to type.

Why is it important to have insects pollinating my apples?

Apples need pollinating insects to transfer pollen between compatible trees. The apple ovary in the centre of the flower has five compartments, each containing two ovules so that up to 10 seeds may develop. The fertilization of every ovule is not essential to fruit development, but usually the more seeds that develop in the apple, the larger it is. About six or seven seeds are necessary for good fruit set.

I've heard that if I plant an apple seed, I won't get the same variety as the original apple. Is this true?

Because an apple variety usually cannot reproduce with itself, the pollen grains that fertilize the seeds will be from a different variety and therefore the seed will not carry the same genetic information as the parent plant. Each apple seed will therefore produce a new variety of apple (a cross between the two parents) which may, or may not, produce a 'tasty' apple. Therefore to get a new tree with the characteristics of the parent, a graft is needed (see page 82).

What is the world's largest nut?

The coco de mer palm (*Lodoicea maldivica*) of the Seychelles is a giant in the plant world. It produces the largest and heaviest seed of any plant on the planet and the male catkins can reach up to a metre (3 feet) in length, making them the longest in the world. The tree can reach nearly 34 metres (100 feet) in height and the mature fruit can be 40 to 50 cm (16 to 20 inches) in diameter, weighing 15 to 30 kilograms (33 to 66 pounds). The fruit requires six to seven years to mature and a further two years to germinate.

Trees AND Water

What is a tree made of?

Between 80 and 90 percent of the bulk of a tree is water, collected from the soil by the tree's roots. The remaining 10 to 20 percent of the tree is made up of carbon and oxygen drawn from the air by the leaves, plus small percentages of nitrogen, potassium, calcium, phosphorus and traces of sulphur, copper, zinc, iron, molybdenum, manganese, cobalt, boron and magnesium.

Do I need to water young trees?

Young, newly planted trees have limited root systems that cannot withstand long periods without adequate soil moisture. Trees that have been in the ground for only a year or two are at greatest risk, but if dry weather continues for long periods, then older trees may also begin to suffer. Signs of drought stress can vary from tree to tree, the most common symptom being wilting of the leaves leading to browning and drying of the entire leaf. The key to successful tree watering is to soak the root system deeply and not to reapply water until the soil starts to dry out. Avoid frequent light applications as this can cause surface rooting and lead to over watering. Young trees, those that have been in the ground for a year or two, should be well soaked once every seven to ten days. Older, more established trees should be deeply watered every two weeks or so.

Opposte: In the course of one summer a large oak tree may use 40,000 litres (8,800 gallons) of water.
Above: Olympic swimming pool – enough water for 80 oak trees for one summer.

At the end of a long, hot summer this sycamore is showing clear signs of stress through drought.

How much water do trees use?

Trees lose water by a process called transpiration (see page 30). An apple tree two metres (6 feet 6 inches) high may use up to 700 litres (155 gallons) of water in a summer. A fully grown birch tree may use 17,000 litres (3,740 gallons) while a large oak may use up to 40,000 litres (8,800 gallons). An Olympic-sized swimming pool contains approximately 3,125,000 litres (687,500 gallons) of water – or enough to keep nearly 80 oak trees going for a summer.

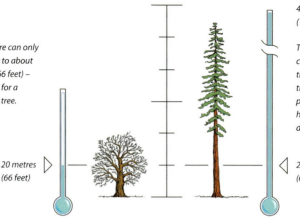

Root pressure can only move water to about 20 metres (66 feet) – not enough for a mature oak tree.

400 metres (1,320 feet)

Tension cohesion could pull water to the top of the tallest trees, but the pressure required has never been demonstrated.

20 metres (66 feet)

20 metres (66 feet)

How do tall trees get water to their tops?

Scientists are not yet really confident that they know the answer. There are two ways in which water appears to move within a tree – being pushed up from below (the root pressure theory), and being pulled up by the loss of water from the leaves (the tension-cohesion theory).

Root pressure

Water is certainly 'pushed up' from the roots in certain trees like birch and maple. In these trees in spring, sugars and minerals are secreted into the xylem (see page 34). This causes water to be sucked into the tubes to dilute the sugar and salts by osmosis, forcing water up the tree. In the USA the rising spring water, sugar and salts (collectively called sap) have been recognised as useful and are collected to make maple syrup, whilst in the UK spring birch sap is used to make birch wine.

Water loss from leaves (tension-cohesion)

It has been known for over a hundred years that water is usually transported under pressure – ie pulled not pushed. The 'pull' in trees is the evaporation of water from the 'stomata' in the leaves (transpiration). This creates reduced pressure in the plant cells around the stomata into which water moves from the xylem tubes. The result is a constant 'pull' (tension) drawing water up the tree. Because water molecules stick together like magnets (cohesion), research has shown that theoretically this would allow water to be pulled 400 metres (1300 feet) or more up a tree (more than sufficient for the tallest trees – currently only 112 metres (370 feet) – see page 42).

This coast redwood, growing in Scotland, is only 42.8 metres (140 feet 5 inches) high, a mere baby by comparison with the current tallest one in the world – 'Hyperion', a massive 115.5 metres (379 feet) – in California.

The problems with the theories opposite are that:

1) root pressure can only move water to about 20 metres (66 feet) up a tree – nothing like enough for the tallest trees on its own.

2) the considerable pressure required for tension-cohesion to draw water up to the tops of the tallest trees has been demonstrated to 'suck' the sides of a tree in during hot days and expand them again at night. Why trees do not simply collapse under the strain of being sucked 'in' and 'out' is not yet fully understood.

3) the theoretical pressure differences required for tension-cohesion to draw water to the tops of trees has not been demonstrated around the trees themselves.

Unfortunately, therefore, there is still no definitive explanation of how water reaches the tops of tall trees.

Roots

What are roots for?

The basic functions of roots (and their fundamental mycorrhizal associations – see page 34) are to allow trees to take up water, to take in mineral nutrients, to move the water and minerals to the tree's trunk and to provide support and anchorage to the tree. Roots also store starch and oils for the tree to use when growing, and produce a range of plant hormones.

How deep do roots go and how far do they spread?

Most trees begin life with a taproot emerging from the seed. This goes straight down into the soil (if possible), then after a few years side roots develop to create a wide-spreading fibrous root system, with mainly horizontal surface roots and only a few vertical, deep roots. A typical mature tree – 30 to 50 metres (100 to 150 feet) tall – has a root system that may extend horizontally in all directions, frequently as far as the tree is tall, but with over 90 percent of the roots in the top 100 cm (40 inches) of soil (rather like a wine glass on a dinner plate – see above). Recent research also suggests that roots can sometimes extend out far beyond the drip line of the canopy. Research at Kew Gardens showed that none of the trees studied (nearly 700 in total, of 36 species) had roots which reached deeper than 3 metres (10 feet) into the soil. Although some trees can have deeper roots, a depth of less than 3 metres (10 feet) is the norm.

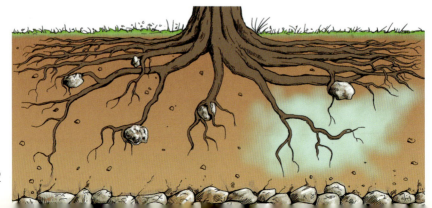

What are aerial roots?

Aerial roots are produced by trees for two reasons: firstly to supplement their food supply and secondly to increase stability. Root cells can only develop in humid conditions so aerial rooting is mainly a phenomenon of tropical or very humid conditions (e.g. the banyan in India and the mangrove in America). Another example is the strangler fig (*Ficus sumatrana*), a parasitic plant of tropical forests that begins life as a seed deposited by birds in the top of a host tree and then sends roots snaking down to the ground. Ancient trees in the British Isles, particularly limes, often develop a sort of aerial root system inside rotting or hollow stems. These aerial roots can recycle the minerals, nutrients and trace elements from the decaying wood of the hollowing trunk of the tree – so the tree is actually recycling itself.

Which trees throw suckers and why?

Suckering is a form of reproduction that does not involve another tree. Some trees can produce new shoots from their root system, which can then grow into new trees – these are called 'root suckers'. The growth of new shoots can be triggered naturally, or as a result of stress: for example, by drought or root damage. Species that produce suckers include elms, poplars, cherries, plums and false acacias.

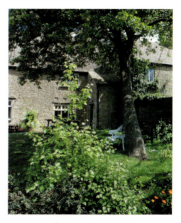

Above: The wild service tree shows its tendency to sucker profusely.

Left: A superb engraving from 1873 shows the amazing aerial roots of the banyan tree.

What is a mycorrhizal relationship?

Mycorrhiza is a symbiotic association between a fungus and the roots of a tree. Often a tree will not grow properly unless the appropriate fungus is present in the soil. Roots colonized by mycorrhizal fungi take up nutrients more efficiently than uncolonized roots. In return, the fungi obtain carbohydrates and selected vitamins from the tree. Mycorrhizal fungi can also protect the roots from colonization by other micro-organisms, some of which may be detrimental to the tree.

How do roots absorb water?

Roots consist of several different parts, each with a distinct function. The big roots you see most easily are part of a complex transportation system. Except for the outer bark-like skin, they are composed of old dysfunctional cells that have been modified into vessels and sieve tubes designed simply to carry liquids. The working root, less easily seen, is the root tip terminating in pale coloured root hairs. This is where water and mineral salts in a weak solution are absorbed from the soil.

Cells known as the phloem contain sugars and starches carried down from the foliage. This sugar-rich solution is diluted by soil water drawn in from outside. That is how water is absorbed. The mineral solution is then transported along the main roots to the tree trunk by xylem cells. At the 'root collar' there is a complicated switching of vessels into the circulatory system of the stem; a sort of 'Clapham Junction of the tree'. It is important never to damage or bury this critical area.

Which trees are suitable to plant near gas pipelines?

Currently National Grid recommends that the only hardwood plants which should be planted directly across pipelines are hedge plants such as hawthorn and blackthorn. These should only be planted where a hedge is necessary either for screening purposes or to indicate a field boundary. Poplar and willow trees should not be planted within 10 metres (30 feet) of the pipeline. Where screening is required, the following are shallow rooting and may be planted over the pipeline, road and field crossings: blackthorn, broom, cotoneaster, elder, hazel, laurel, privet, hawthorn, snowberry and most ornamental shrubs. Christmas trees (*Picea abies*) may be planted to within 3 metres (10 feet) of the pipeline. Permission to plant is given on the strict understanding that they are clear-felled at intervals not exceeding seven years.

The roots of a tree 20 metres (60 feet) tall, which had grown around a medium pressure gas main.

What damage can trees do to underground gas pipelines?

Trees can have a detrimental effect on underground gas pipelines in several ways. Tree roots may affect some types of pipe coatings. This occurs when the root grows between the steel of the pipeline and the corrosion resistant coating, causing them to separate and allow water to seep in.

When large trees growing over the pipeline are blown over in gales, the pull of the root system may induce undesirable stresses on the pipeline. Problems may also occur in drought conditions, in clay soils, where the trees pull the water out of the soils and sub soils causing the ground to shrink. This ground movement can damage iron gas mains, resulting in a leak.

Tree roots can also cause direct physical damage to the older cast iron gas distribution mains by growing into the pipeline joints. Councils and developers should therefore check the location of underground services before planting new trees.

Bark

What is bark for?

Bark is the outermost layer of a tree. It overlays the wood (see page 15) and is made up of the inner 'phloem' which carries sugar around the tree and the 'outer bark' which acts like a waterproof skin. Part of the outer bark layer is filled with air, tannin and/or waxy substances and is called the 'phelloderm' layer. The purpose of the 'phelloderm' is to provide protection against damage, pests and diseases, as well as dehydration and extreme temperatures. In some trees the 'phelloderm' layer has become substantially thicker, to protect the tree from fire or dehydration (e.g. cork oak and giant redwood).

What is cork?

Cork is the 'phelloderm' layer of the bark of the cork oak (*Quercus suber*), a medium sized, evergreen tree from southwest Europe and northwest Africa. The bark of this species grows thick and 'corky' and is harvested every 10 to 12 years. After cutting the cork re-grows before being harvested again. Annually the European cork industry produces over 300,000 tonnes with a value of €1.5 billion and it employs 30,000 people. Most of the revenue for this industry comes from wine production although it uses only 15 percent of the annual cork production. The remainder of the crop is used for insulation, flooring and other domestic uses.

GATHERING THE BARK OF THE CORK-TREE.

Right: The Clapton Court Ash, the largest ash in the country, whose real girth is massively increased by a huge burr which covers the entire base of the tree. Below: The spiral pattern of sweet chestnut bark.

Why does the bark of old sweet chestnut trees spiral?

Spiralling occurs in many, probably most, trees to some extent. Foresters suggest that spiral grain is caused by sap taking a spiral course during growth. In silver fir great spiral cracks sometimes snake up a stem in hot dry conditions. Old chestnuts can spiral in either direction or go more or less straight up. Spiralling is a feature of young trees too but it is more visible in old trees because the bark is vertically ridged – more so in sweet chestnuts than most other trees in Britain.

What is a burr?

A burr is an outgrowth on a tree. One possible explanation is that burrs may result from damage to the tree by browsing animals such as deer, while another is that they may be caused by insects or viruses attacking the tree. Burrs may also be the development of a mass of buds buried in the bark – called epicormic buds. These epicormic buds are a form of insurance policy for the tree, allowing the development of new branches if the tree's crown becomes damaged. If the buds develop and grow as clusters the extra wood they produce can generate burrs.

Fossil  trees

Above: Britain's record girth ginkgo.
Right: Delicate fronds of dawn redwood.
Below: Amber with insect inclusion.

Why are some trees called fossil trees?

Trees known as 'fossil trees' are those discovered initially as fossils. Some have subsequently been found to be still in existence, often in an apparently unchanged state. For example, the ginkgo tree first appeared in the fossil record of 200 million years ago and was naturally abundant throughout Britain 60 million years ago, before it disappeared from these islands. The species was then re-introduced to Britain in 1754 and is now found widely planted in parks, gardens and streets.

Other examples of such trees are the dawn redwood, known from the fossil records but not discovered living until 1941, and the recently discovered wollemi pine in Australia – known from 90 million-year-old fossils, but only recorded alive in 1994 in a valley in New South Wales, Australia.

What is coal?

Coal is compressed carbon from forest swamps that covered large areas of Britain including 2,600 square kilometres (1,000 square miles) in one part of Wales, in the Upper Carboniferous period 255 to 220 million years ago. Whole regions of the Northern Hemisphere began to sink during that period. Vegetation built up in these basins until further subsidence caused inundation by fresh water or the sea. Alluvium carried in the water formed bands of grit, shale, mudstone and limestone interspersed with coal seams. Plant life in the coal forests consisted of 30 metres (100 feet) tall scale-trees (*Lycopods*) and a shrub layer of fern-like plants, horsetails and creepers. One horsetail (*Calamites*) produced trees 15 metres (50 feet) tall. Trees with strap-like leaves (*Cordaites*) had winged seeds borne in open cones. These were the primitive ancestors of conifers.

Why do conifers produce resin?

Conifers produce resins for various reasons which include sealing the plant's wounds as a defence against insects and perhaps some fungi. Resin has value for its chemical constituents and is used for varnishes and adhesives. Formed in special resin canals, it is typically exuded in soft drops from wounds, hardening into solid masses in the air. Perhaps the most famous of all resins is amber.

What is amber?

Amber is a fossilised resin much used for the manufacture of ornamental objects. Most of the world's amber is in the range of 30 to 90 million years old and a large percentage comes from the Baltic. Baltic amber is thought to have come from a now extinct pine called *Pinus succinifera*. Many insects, spiders, crustaceans and other small organisms have been found trapped in the amber, having been enveloped while the resin was liquid.

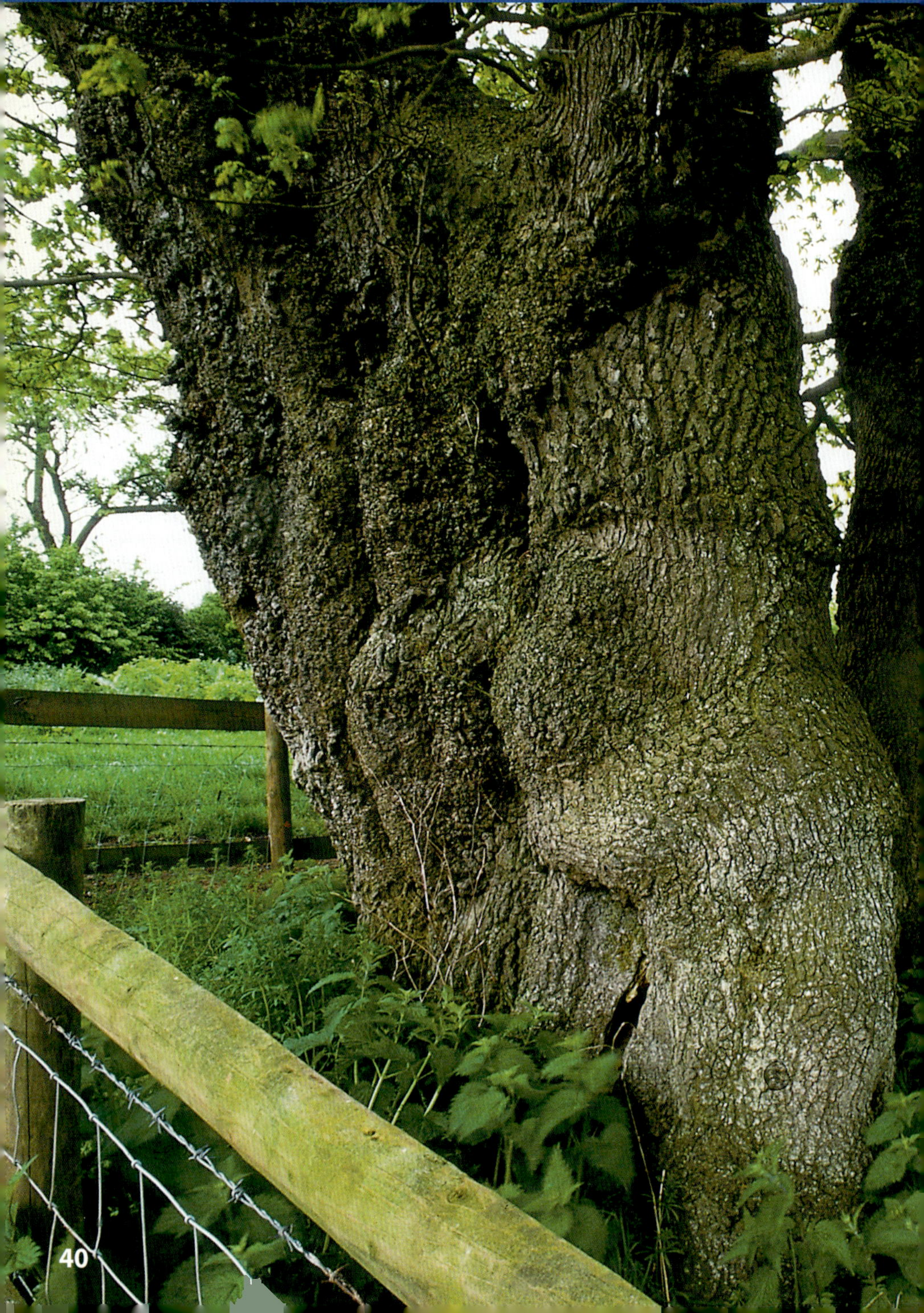

World Record Breakers

Which is currently the world's tallest tree?

During the summer of 2006, researchers from the Humboldt State University discovered the tallest recorded tree in the world, a coast redwood (*Sequoia sempervirens*), which they named 'Hyperion'. This tree is 115.5 metres (379.1 feet) tall, beating the previous record holder, the 112.9 metre (370.5 feet) tall 'Stratosphere Giant'.

The researchers were exploring rugged areas of the Redwood National and State Parks in the USA and also found two other redwoods taller than the 'Stratosphere Giant'. This suggests that there may have been many other massive redwoods before the commercial logging of the area was stopped in 1978.

Which was the world's tallest tree ever?

The tallest tree ever recorded was an Australian mountain ash (*Eucalyptus regnans*) in Victoria, southeastern Australia. It was named the 'Ferguson Tree' after the government surveyor, William Ferguson, who measured it in 1872 at 133 metres (436 feet), though this figure is now debated.

Where is the deepest recorded root system?

There are records in areas of extremely limited rainfall of trees producing deep roots. One root from a wild fig tree has penetrated 120 metres (394 feet) into Echo Caves near Ohrigstad, South Africa.

Which is the world's most massive tree?

The tree with the largest volume in the world is a giant redwood (*Sequoiadendron giganteum*) growing in the Sequoia National Park, California. It was discovered in 1879. Now known as 'General Sherman', it is 83.82 metres (275 feet) tall and has a girth of 31.3 metres (102 feet). Its 1,487 cubic metres (52,508 cubic feet) of trunk is enough to make five billion matches.

*Right: The 'General Sherman'
is the most massive tree in
the world.*

CHESTNUT-TREE OF A HUNDRED HORSES, MOUNT ETNA.

This engraving from 1873 shows the sweet chestnut on Mount Etna which had the greatest ever recorded girth. The tree survives to this day, but only as three fragments of the original bole.

Which is the world's rarest tree?

There are several trees of which only one known specimen exists in the world, including the caffe marron (*Ramosmania heterophylla*) from the island of Rodrigues and the *Pennantia baylisiana* on Great Island in the Three Kings Islands Group, New Zealand.

Which is the world's slowest growing tree?

A white cedar (*Thuja occidentalis*) growing near the Canadian Great Lakes has reached a height of only 10.2 cm (4 inches) after 155 years.

Which tree has the largest canopy?

The canopy of a great banyan (*Ficus benghalensis*) – which has been growing in the Indian Botanical Garden, Calcutta, since 1787 – measures 412 metres (1,350 feet) in circumference and covers 1.2 hectares (3 acres) The tree's canopy is propped up by 1,775 supporting roots.

Which tree has the greatest girth recorded?

A sweet chestnut (*Castanea sativa*), known as 'The Tree of a Hundred Horses', growing on Linguaglossa Road in Sant Alfio, on the eastern slope of Mount Etna in Sicily. The tree had a circumference of 57.9 metres (190 feet) when measured in 1780. It has now split into three parts.

This aspen 'woodland' in South Wales covers more than 0.4 hectares (1 acre) and consists of over 1,000 stems. It is one tree and remarkable in the UK, but is extremely modest compared to the record breaking aspen in America which covers 43 hectares (106 acres).

Which tree has the earliest known planting date?

The Bo tree (*Ficus religiosa*) at Anuradhapura in Sri Lanka is believed to have been planted around 300 BC. This tree is thought to have grown from a cutting taken from the tree under which the Buddha found enlightenment.

What is the longest living type of tree in the world?

The aspen can be up to 10,000 years old and is one of the oldest living organisms on Earth. The best demonstration of its longevity is in North America where huge swathes survive exactly as they have since the last Ice Age. The surface roots continually throw up suckers, constantly increasing the tree's territory with new replacement stems (but still the same original tree). Fire helps aspen in this quest for space. In winter when the ground is frozen or wet, the roots survive forest fires and send up new sucker shoots. In summer, when dry ground and the aspen roots in it are burned, another part of the extensive root system will usually survive and recolonize. One aspen (*Populus tremuloides*) in the Wasatch Mountains, Utah, USA, is thought to cover an area of 43 hectares (106 acres), growing originally from a single rootstock.

Where is the world's tallest and longest hedge?

The world's tallest and longest hedge is the Meikleour Beech Hedge in Perthshire, Scotland, planted in 1746. Its tapered height varies from 24.4 metres (80 feet) to 36.6 metres (120 feet) along its full length of 550 metres (1,804 feet). The hedge is trimmed once every 10 years.

Which tree has the highest ring count?

The highest number of rings ever found on a tree is 4,862. They were found by Donald Graybill of the University of Arizona in a bristlecone pine (*Pinus longeava*) known as 'Prometheus', which was cut down on 6 August 1964 on Mount Wheeler, Nevada, USA. The tree was cut by Donald R. Currey, a graduate student at the University of North Carolina studying the Little Ice Age using dendrochronology techniques.

Where is the world's largest forest?

The Taiga or boreal forest is a transcontinental belt of coniferous forest that encircles the northern hemisphere. It reaches across Alaska to Russia. The once-forested highlands of Scotland can also be included in this belt. It is the largest terrestrial habitat on Earth,

The tallest and longest hedge in the world at Meikleour in Perthshire.

Vast Montezuma bald cypress at Oaxaca in Mexico.

making up one third of the world's forested land and covering some 15 million square kilometres (equivalent to 42 times the size of Germany). About 60 percent of this area is in Russia, 30 percent in Canada and 10 percent is shared between Alaska, the Baltic States, Scotland and Scandinavia.

Which is the oldest living individual tree?

The oldest living individual tree is said to be a bristlecone pine (*Pinus longaeva*), nicknamed 'Methuselah' (after Methuselah, the longest-lived person in the Bible). The tree, which stands in the Bristlecone Pine Forest in the White Mountains of eastern California, was found by Dr Edmund Schulman (USA) in 1957 who estimated it to be 4,600 years old.

Which tree has the widest tree trunk in the world?

In Santa Maria del Tule, Oaxaca, Mexico, there is a Montezuma bald cypress (*Taxodium mucronatum*). It is approximately 11.4 metres (37 feet 6 inches) in diameter, approximately 43 metres (141 feet) tall and over 2,000 years old. Because the trunk of the tree is not circular but has a distorted and irregular shape, it is not possible to calculate its circumference (girth) with any accuracy.

It was thought that the tree comprised several different individual trees that had merged together. An examination of DNA samples taken from the trunks in 1996 showed that they all came from a single tree.

British Record Breakers

Which is the oldest tree in Britain?

Estimated to be perhaps 5,000 years old, the Fortingall Yew (*Taxus baccata*) stands at the geographical heart of Scotland. It is believed to be the most ancient tree in Britain. The tree was first described in 1769 by the Hon. Daines Barrington, who measured it as 16 metres (52 feet) in circumference. Today this venerable tree is still a very impressive sight and is enclosed within a wall built to create a sanctuary for its undisturbed growth.

Which is the tallest tree in Britain?

The choice of tree considered to be the tallest in Britain has varied over a number of years between a Douglas fir (*Pseudotsuga menziesii*) in Reeling Glen Woods, Invernesshire and a Douglas fir at Powis Castle, Wales. The Powis Castle tree had briefly held the title when it was found to be 63 metres (205 feet) tall, but when a BBC film crew arrived at the Reeling Glen tree in 2006 with officials of the Tree Register of the British Isles, they used the latest laser technology and found that it was just over 65 metres (210 feet) tall, making it currently the tallest recorded tree in Britain.

Which is the biggest tree in Britain?

A giant sweet chestnut (*Castanea sativa*) in Penshurst, Kent is the largest living tree on record in Britain. It has a height of 32 metres (104 feet) and a circumference of 16 metres (52 feet). It was coppiced 300 years ago, which resulted in seven huge stems, and has long been known as the 'Seven Sisters'.

The biggest tree in Britain is this massive sweet chestnut, known as the 'Seven Sisters', near Penshurst in Kent.

Which is the smallest tree in Britain?

The smallest trees in Britain are the dwarf willows (dwarf willow, mountain willow and woolly willow) that grow on hillsides at an altitude usually above 610 metres (2,000 feet). These trees are often no more than 6 cm (2.4 in) tall.

Which is the fastest growing tree in Britain?

Leyland cypress (× *Cupressocyparis leylandii*) is a cross between Nootka cypress (*Xanthocyparis nootkatensis*) and Monterey cypress (*Cupressus macrocarpa*). The Leyland cypress is Britain's fastest growing tree, growing up to a metre (over 3 feet) per year and reaching to date heights of up to 36 metres (118 feet).

Which is the slowest growing native tree in Britain?

Box (*Buxus sempervirens*) is a small tree that grows in the harsh conditions of the chalk and limestone soils in southern England. It tolerates shade well and other faster growing species usually overtake it, with the result that box becomes the canopy on steep hill slopes only where competitive trees cannot become established. Because box is so slow growing, its grain is very fine, making the wood very hard and extremely valuable. Indeed, boxwood can be the hardest wood of any European tree when grown slowly, and is so dense that it will even sink in water when newly cut and green.

What is the rarest native tree in Britain?

The rarest trees in Britain are in the Sorbus family, which consists of three widespread species: the whitebeam (*Sorbus aria*), the rowan (*Sorbus aucuparia*) and the wild service tree (*Sorbus tormentalis*) plus 16 other species of which 15 are endemic (i.e. found growing naturally only in Britain).

Of these endemic trees the rarest is Ley's whitebeam (*Sorbus leyana*) – which is confined to two carboniferous limestone crags in Brecon, and whose total known world population does not appear to exceed 16 trees in the wild.

Right: Britain's rarest native tree is the Ley's whitebeam, growing on cliffs above the Taff Valley.

Trees and Woodlands

What percentage of Britain is covered in trees and how does this compare with the rest of Europe?

The Countryside Surveys of Great Britain and Northern Ireland estimate that woodland covers nearly 12 per cent of the UK. By comparison, 28 per cent of France is wooded, 29 per cent of Spain, 30 per cent of Germany and 33 per cent of Italy and Greece. Indeed, in Europe, only Ireland and Iceland have a lower woodland cover than Britain. Along with the woodland cover the UK also still has many trees remaining as in-field trees especially in parklands and wood pastures and in our extensive hedge network plus many trees in our parks and gardens.

How much woodland is there in Britain?

The stock of broadleaved woodland in the UK increased by about five percent since 1990 to around 1.5 million hectares (3.7 million acres) in 1998. The national expansion of coniferous woodland over previous decades came to a halt in the 1990s at around 1.4 million hectares (3.5 million acres). This represents 11.6 percent of the land area.

What is the difference between forest and woodland?

There are two uses of the word forest in the UK.

- In Medieval England the term 'Forest' was a designation used for an area where the king or other eminent person had the right to hunt deer. 'Forest' was a legal term and did not mean that the whole area was wooded; indeed, there was no direct reference to trees or woodland. It was rather that the king had taken it upon himself to use the land in order to protect deer and, by default, other wildlife for the royal hunt.

- More recently a forest has come to mean a large area with a high density of trees – and this is the more common understanding of the word today. These plant communities cover large areas of the globe.

How many trees are there in Britain?

There are an estimated 123 million live trees outside woodland in Britain. Including all trees in woodland and forests, there are an estimated 4 billion trees in Britain.

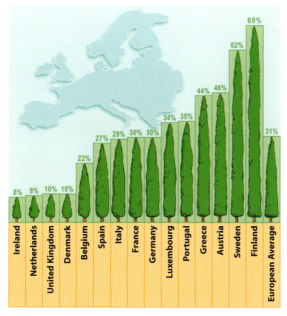

Ireland 8%
Netherlands 9%
United Kingdom 10%
Denmark 10%
Belgium 22%
Spain 27%
Italy 29%
France 30%
Germany 30%
Luxembourg 34%
Portugal 35%
Greece 44%
Austria 46%
Sweden 62%
Finland 69%
European Average 31%

Distribution map of tree cover across Europe.

What is the National Forest?

In the late 1980s, it was decided to transform an area of 520 square kilometres (200 square miles) in the centre of England into a new multi-purpose forest. The site chosen for 'The National Forest' linked the ancient forests of Needwood and Charnwood and was symbolically central in the UK, spanning three counties in the English Midlands – Derbyshire, Leicestershire and Staffordshire. From one of the country's least wooded regions (at 6 percent), the ambitious goal for The National Forest is to increase woodland cover to about a third of all the land within its boundary. By 2005, the woodland cover of the designated area had increased to 16 percent.

How many Royal Hunting 'Forests' were historically recorded?

There were over 130 different forests recorded through history, some large and famous like the New Forest in Hampshire, Sherwood Forest in Nottinghamshire and the Forest of Dean in Gloucestershire, whose boundaries are still known and where much of the original landscape still remains. Others, like the Forests of Buckholt, Cantrelly and Char (Hampshire), have been lost and remain only as small woodlands.

Hedges
in Britain

What is the total length of hedges in Britain?

In England and Wales there are approximately half a million kilometres (312,000 miles) of hedge or remnant hedge. There are also approximately 24,000 kilometres (15,000 miles) of hedge in Scotland and 118,000 kilometres (74,000 miles) in Northern Ireland.

Changes in farm management now mean that hedges are being cut less often. Is this a good or a bad thing?

There are two excellent reasons for not cutting a hedge every year.

The first is that most tree and shrub flowers are produced on year-old twigs. Annual cutting removes these twigs, so there are fewer flowers, berries and nuts. This has a big impact on a wide range of wildlife, from insects like butterflies and moths, through birds like thrushes (especially redwings and fieldfares) to mammals like dormice. Only late flowering species (e.g. brambles, roses and other climbers) produce good fruit crops in hedges that are cut every year.

The second reason is that the bigger a hedge, the more wildlife it will support. For example, it is estimated that for every year a hedge is left uncut it will gain two species of breeding bird, whilst some insects like the brown hairstreak butterfly that is heavily dependent on hedges, only lay their eggs on the new year's growth, which is destroyed by cutting. Clearly, if this new growth is cut off each autumn or winter the eggs will all perish, explaining why the butterfly is now rare.

What shape and size of hedge is particularly good for wildlife?

The wider and taller a hedge, the more wildlife it is likely to support: many species show a strong preference for larger hedges. Turtle doves and dormice, for example, prefer hedges that are at least 4 metres (13 feet) high. It has been estimated that for every 2 square metres (22 square feet) increase in cross-sectional area, one more bird species will breed. Hedges that have been allowed to develop into lines of trees probably support the most wildlife of all, particularly if they remain bushy at the base. A few species, however, like yellowhammers, whitethroats and partridges, prefer short hedges, so a few such hedges on a farm are beneficial.

Top: A well-maintained hedge, trimmed in the 'A' shape, with a good spread of hedge trees.

Above: A brown hairstreak butterfly – a hedge specialist.

At what time of year should a hedge be cut?

Hedge cutting should always avoid the bird breeding season, 1 March to 31 July. The occupied nests of all wild birds are protected under law. It is an offence intentionally or recklessly to damage a nest while it is in use or being built. This applies even to 'pest species' like magpies, crows and woodpigeons, except where permitted under general licence from the Department for Environment, Food and Rural Affairs (Defra).

Nearly every hedge in the country will have birds breeding in it in the spring and early summer. Since it is highly likely to damage nests or at least cause the birds to desert, cutting the hedge between 1 March and 31 July is regarded as bad practice. It is best to cut hedges outside the breeding season, in the late winter (January to February) so that the berry crop remains available to birds for as long as possible. If ground conditions and cropping patterns make this difficult, then cutting should be carried out as late as possible.

Why are hedges and hedge trees important?

Hedges and hedge trees are extremely important places for wildlife because they offer a wide diversity of habitats in a relatively small area. Hedges can provide shelter, breeding opportunities, nesting sites, song posts, hiding places and ecologically-friendly links between habitats.

The biological value of hedges and hedge trees to Britain's wildlife is immense. The UK Biodiversity Group has recorded over 600 plant species, 1,500 insect species, 65 bird species and 20 mammal species living in hedges at some time. There are even 13 species of plants and animals presently occurring in British hedges which are globally threatened or rapidly declining. Many of the trees in our hedges are mature, veteran or ancient and they contribute significantly to the landscape character of an area. In the past hedge trees such as pollards (see page 67) were an extremely valuable sustainable resource and where they remain they are part of our living cultural heritage.

Left: Hedge trimmers with mechanical flails should take particular care to avoid young hedge trees.

Above: A young hedge sapling, like this, is the future for Britain's hedge trees.

Why do farmers not leave more saplings to become hedge trees?

Hedge trees can cost a farmer money and provide little if any income. The costs of hedge cutting can be increased by the extra time and effort needed to avoid trees which may also shade out crops and grass, so causing further economic loss.

Collectively, these factors add up to reasons why some farmers don't encourage more hedge trees. Currently, there are also no grants available to farmers for planting new hedge trees or for maintaining those that already exist.

The fact there are so many hedge trees left and that some new ones are being planted or left to grow on is proof that many farmers are prepared to look after the environment even where it costs them money.

Native, Naturalised & Introduced

How many tree species grow in Britain?

Britain has excellent growing conditions for trees, the warm maritime climate allowing a huge range to flourish on our islands. Indeed, it has been said that Britain's climate makes it one of the most favourable temperate places in the world to grow a wide range of trees. As a result there are many thousands of tree species and varieties growing throughout Britain. Some are widely planted, while others occur in just a few specialist gardens and nurseries.

What is the difference between 'native' and 'non-native' tree species?

The term 'native tree' is used to describe species that have colonized the British Isles naturally: that is, without human interference (see page 10). These are generally taken to be those trees that arrived naturally after the last Ice Age (c10,000 years ago) and before these islands were cut off from the rest of Europe by the rising sea levels (c5,000 years ago). 'Non-native' trees, by comparison, are species that have been introduced into the country by human action.

Two of Britain's most familiar naturalised species – the horse chestnut (opposite) and the sweet chestnut (right).

What are 'naturalised' trees?

Naturalised trees are non-native species that are now found in the wild as self-sustaining populations – growing and reproducing successfully of their own accord. Examples include sweet chestnut (introduced by the Romans) and horse chestnut (introduced in 1616).

Does it matter whether a tree is a native or not?

To environmentalists, native species are generally considered preferable to non-natives, as they provide habitats for many species of wildlife that have become adapted over thousand years to live within their structures. For example, during the last 30 years, strenuous efforts have been made to eradicate 'non-native' tree species that occupy space where more wildlife-rich broadleaf trees could grow.

In an urban setting, however, where non-native species may have a better chance of survival because of the more difficult conditions, the debate about native or non-native is much more difficult. Here the qualities that the tree brings to the space and its ability to thrive are often more important than the fact that it may support more limited wildlife, and under these circumstances a non-native tree is often the better choice.

All ancient trees are important, especially for their biodiversity and heritage value. Exotic veteran trees can also be very valuable for wildlife, especially where they are near to ancient native trees; for example in parkland.

What is an 'invasive species'?

The term 'invasive species' is applied to non-native trees which spread rapidly and displace native vegetation in an uncontrolled manner. They include rhododendron which has huge impact on the local ecology.

Is sycamore a native species?

The sycamore (*Acer pseudoplatanus*) was first written about in England by Lyte in 1578, although there is a carving in Christ Church, Oxford on a shrine to St Frideswide which includes leaves and seeds of sycamore and which is dated 1289, suggesting that the species has been in Britain longer than people imagine. The first recorded sycamores in Scotland include a tree near Dunblane,

described in 1842 as 440 years old; another in Largs planted by Sir Andrew Wood in 1497; and one in the grounds of Newbattle Abbey, on the outskirts of Dalkeith, thought to have been planted around 1550.

Recently, however, the debate on whether the sycamore is a native or non-native tree has been re-opened. Sycamore is now so widely distributed in Britain that only ash and hawthorn are more widespread and it is found higher up on hillsides than any broadleaf except rowan. Sycamore also now represents 8.8 per cent of the total of British woodlands with increasing importance towards the west and the north of the country. Unfortunately its low insect species-richness, invasive potential, and heavy honeydew production gave sycamore a poor reputation. However, sycamore produces high quality timber and provides an important food source for some species of invertebrates (e.g. bees) and for some migrating birds. Therefore perhaps the debate over 'natural or not' is irrelevant and the question should perhaps be 'is sycamore valuable in the countryside?' to which the answer is probably a cautious 'yes'.

Are native trees always best in a community planting?

If the theme of a particular community planting requires native species or it is a condition for grant aid then so be it, but the trees you plant may not be as 'native' as you think. Very few so-called British native trees are entirely British at all. Trees worldwide have endured a long history of human interference and for hundreds of years alien plants have been brought into the British Isles for all kinds of reasons. English elm, for example, was imported by Neolithic farmers for fodder and cattle bedding.

Above: The Newbattle Abbey Sycamore, an important tree, sadly lost to gales in May 2006.
Opposite: Carvings of sycamore leaves on the 13th century St Frideswide's Shrine in Christ Church, Oxford.

How can I identify a tree?

The best way is to consult a key-based and preferably well-illustrated textbook. Try to break down the options available to avoid having to look through all 2,500 tree species found in the British Isles. Ask yourself, is it a conifer or is it a broadleaved tree? Has it opposite or alternate leaves? Is it evergreen or deciduous? If flowers or fruit are present identification may become easier. Another approach is to ask other people. If a neighbour has a tree like yours ask them if they know what it is. Visit an arboretum or botanic garden to find a labelled specimen of the same kind of tree or ask a member of staff for help. Do not, however, walk around with an armful of foliage, even if it is your own! Take photographs instead.

Is it sessile or English oak?

The distinguishing characteristics of English or pedunculate oak (*Quercus robur*) are leaves with short 5 mm (0.2 inches) stalks and basal ear-like lobes (auricles). The acorns are stalked (the peduncle) – with up to four acorns on each peduncle. By comparison, pure sessile oak (*Quercus petraea*) has larger leaves with longer stalks, 10 to 20 mm (0.4 to 0.8 inches) and no auricles. The acorns are stalkless. Each species can be identified in winter by its fallen stalked, or un-stalked, acorn cups. Hybrids occasionally occur (*Quercus × rosacea*) but confusing variants of the two oaks are more likely to be found.

Left: Sessile oak acorns.
Above: Pedunculate oak acorns.

What is a Lucombe oak?

The Lucombe oak (*Quercus × hispanica*) is a natural hybrid between cork oak (*Quercus suber*) and Turkey oak (*Quercus cerris*). The nature of the hybrids is variable and the trees can exhibit a variety of characteristics of both parents. The tree takes its name from William Lucombe, who found one growing in his nursery in Exeter around 1762. The hybrid between the species is frequent in the wild in south-west Europe and can be found growing in Britain, particularly in the south-west where it was first recorded.

Above: The record girth Turkey oak in Britain, one of the parents of the Lucombe oak (left).

WALNUT-TREE.

What are the key dates of introduction to Britain of the common non-native trees?

Roman introductions
1st – 4th century AD – stone pine, sweet chestnut, walnut, (English elm?) and possibly medlar, mulberry and fig (evidence of the last three has been found in a few Roman sites, but whether they were planting the trees or eating imported fruit is uncertain).

There is then a large historical gap until written evidence begins. Then:

16th century or earlier – sycamore (see page 58), black and white mulberry, holm oak, oriental plane, white poplar, tamarisk, judas tree, laburnum.

17th century – Norway spruce, European larch, tulip tree, false acacia, horse chestnut (1616), Norway maple (1638), swamp cypress (c1640), cedar of Lebanon (1646), red maple (1656), London plane (1680).

18th century – copper beech, Indian bean tree (1726), weeping willow (1730), Turkey oak (1735), tree of heaven (1751), ginkgo (1754), Corsican pine (1758), zelkova (1760), golden rain tree (1763), rhododendron (*ponticum*) (1763), cricket bat willow (1780), Irish yew (c1780), Monkey puzzle (1795)

19th century – Douglas fir (1827), deodar cedar (1830), noble fir (1830), grand fir (1830), Sitka spruce (1831), Monterey pine (1831), coast redwood (1843), giant redwood (1853), katsura tree (1864), Leyland cypress (natural hybrid found in Welshpool in 1888).

20th century – dawn redwood (1941), various eucalyptus.

21st century – Wollemi pine (2004). For a list of native trees – i.e. those that arrived naturally more than 5,000 years ago (see page 11).

From left to right: The walnut (from an 1873 wood engraving), oriental plane, Norway maple, Indian bean tree, giant redwood and deodar cedar.

Tree Management

Huge old small-leaved lime coppice stool.

What is coppicing?

Coppicing is a traditional method of woodland management by which young trees are cut down to near the ground. In the past, before the introduction of chainsaws, the hand cutting would have been by billhook and it is unlikely that the stools would have been cut close to the ground. The re-growth emerges as many new shoots, which can be harvested for poles or firewood. After a number of years (depending on the species cut), the cycle begins again and the coppiced tree or stool is ready to be harvested again.

Typically coppice woodland is cut in sections, rotationally. This ensures that a crop is available each year. The side-effect of the rotational cutting is that a rich variety of habitats is created, as the woodland always has a range of differently aged regrowth in it. This is beneficial for the woodland's wildlife. The length of the cutting cycle depends on the species and the local conditions, and the use to which the product is put. Hazel is usually cut on a seven to nine-year cycle and birch on a three to four-year cycle, whereas oak is coppiced on a 20-year cycle.

Can trees be planted under electricity lines?

To avoid problems if you are planning to plant a new tree or landscaping scheme, you should ensure that you do not plant species that, when mature, would grow into the electrical safety zone or could fall on to the overhead line and cause a fault. Contact the electricity company responsible for the overhead line for advice.

A National Grid electricity line with managed woodland beneath.

Why are trees and hedge managed near electricity cables?

Electricity distribution and transmission companies have to ensure the security of supply and safety to the public, and that overhead lines are kept clear of vegetation. If a branch gets too close to a high voltage power line, the electrical current can 'arc' across from the line to the branch leading to a flashover – potentially causing loss of supply, a fire in the tree or the tree conducting electricity to the ground. Vegetation is therefore managed to ensure that trees do not infringe the electrical safety zone over a number of growing seasons.

What is a maiden?
What is a standard?
Are they different?

A tree which has grown naturally from seed is called a maiden tree. Historically a standard is a maiden tree standing in coppice woodland. Therefore a standard is a maiden, but a maiden is not always a standard (i.e. it could be growing somewhere other than in coppice).

Another use of the word standard is in the horticultural trade where it means a tree of 2 - 3.5 metres (6 - 11 feet) tall.

Above: A black poplar maiden. Opposite: A black poplar pollard.

What is pollarding?

Historically, pollarding is the rotational cutting of trees to encourage the growth of branches by cutting off a tree's stem, two metres (6 feet) or so above ground level. The repeat cutting led to either an expanded 'fist-shape' (bolling) at the top of the trunk or at the end of the cut limbs. Multiple shoots would grow from the bolling. This practice was common in wood-pasture where grazing animals were present. Pollarding above head height protected valuable timber or poles from being damaged by browsing animals such as cattle, horses or deer.

The other use of pollarding was in hedges. In tenanted farms the wood from a tree was the property of the farm owner, but the arisings from a tree – the branches and other produce – were the property of the tenant. Therefore most tenants pollarded all their hedge trees to ensure that they obtained the maximum amount of 'arisings' from each tree for fodder or firewood.

Where old pollards are a long time out of their cutting rotation they are called lapsed pollards and it is advisable to take professional advice before attempting restoration cutting of these trees. The aim would be to avoid the collapse of the trees and not to restore the original cutting regime down as far as the bolling.

Why are urban trees pollarded?

Pollarding is often used in urban areas to reduce a tree's size or for health and safety reasons. It prevents the tree from becoming too large for its space and reduces the risk of falling branches that could harm property and people. Once cut the tree will grow a new crown.

TREES IN THE ENVIRONMENT

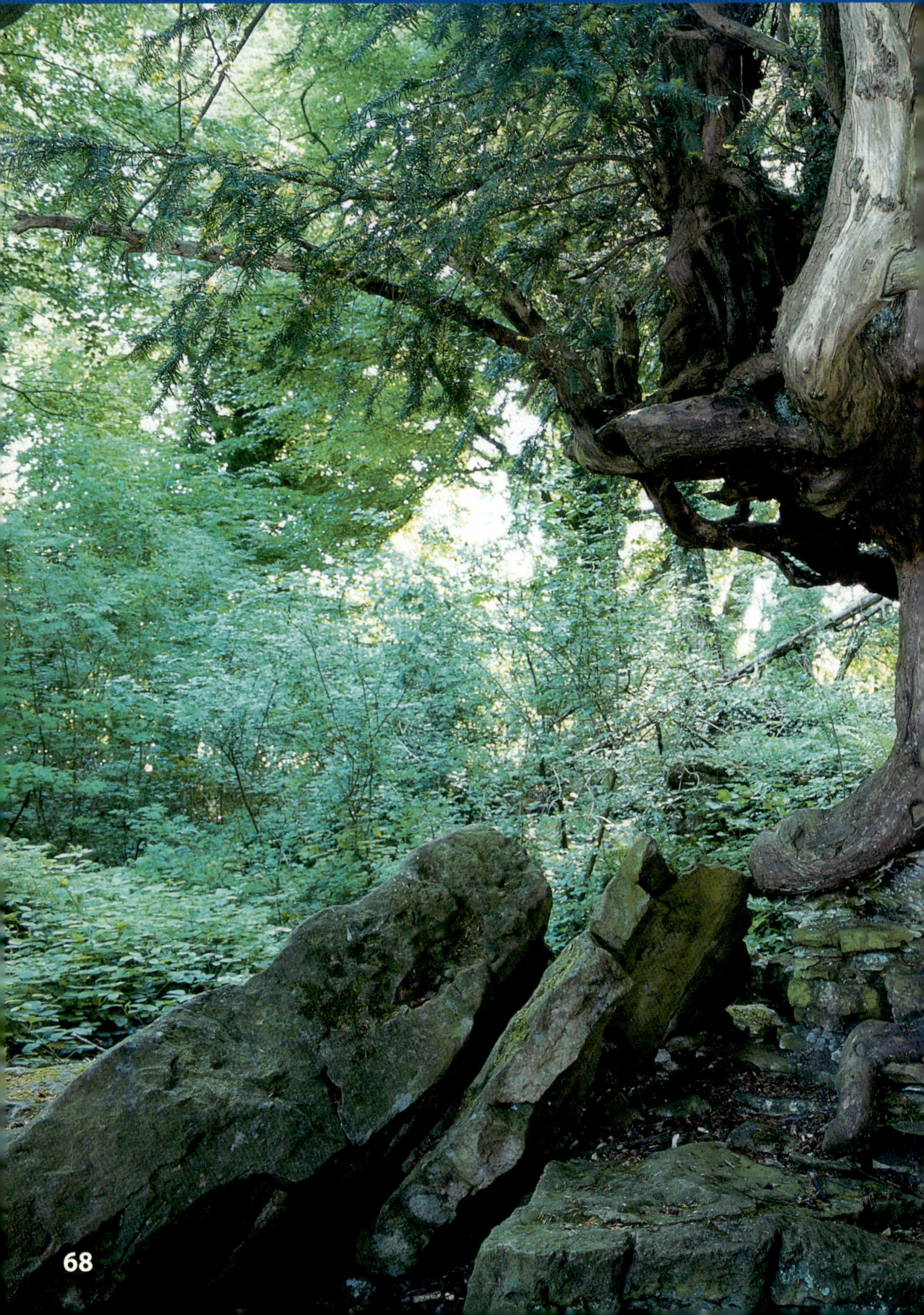

Colonization of trees

Does mistletoe harm trees?

Mistletoe is an evergreen hemi-parasitic plant, growing on the branches of a wide variety of deciduous trees. Although it is most commonly seen growing on old apple trees, it is also frequently found on lime, ash and poplar trees.

Spread by birds, the white berries are coated with a sticky gum which hardens and attaches the seed firmly to its future host. The seed then produces a 'root', which pierces the bark and secures the new mistletoe plant firmly in the growing wood. Mistletoe's evergreen leaves undertake their own photosynthesis, although the plant relies on the tree mainly for minerals and water. The consequences of a heavy infestation of mistletoe can eventually prove fatal to a tree, but usually it only causes a slight reduction in growth.

Despite the problems mistletoe can cause to the tree, recent studies have shown that it has a wide range of ecological values, from food for wildlife to excellent locations for roosting and nesting. Therefore, on balance, mistletoe should not be eradicated without good reason (e.g. safety).

How many species of mistletoe are there?

Out of 1,350 species of mistletoe worldwide, only one (*Viscum album*) grows in Europe, mostly on lime, oak and apple. A subspecies in Central Europe grows on pine and fir trees.

Apple tree festooned with mistletoe.

Rowan growing from within a large ash tree.

Why does mistletoe only grow on certain trees – and which ones?

The occurrence of mistletoe is restricted because it is so fastidious. The bark on which a seed is deposited must be rough enough to hold it firmly in place but not so thick that the developing root cannot penetrate it. Only a small number of trees have this (usually in their upper branches) and also have cambium that is compatible with the future nutritional needs of mistletoe.

Trees that are suitable include lime, apple, hawthorn, occasionally oak and some poplar, but not British native black poplar or the grey or white species. Natural distribution in the British Isles is limited to broad bands from Devon to Bristol and up the lower Severn Valley; from Dorset to Suffolk, with frequent patches to the south of that line; and from London sporadically to York.

Why do some trees grow on others?

In Britain there are no parasitic trees, mistletoe being the nearest thing we have to a woody parasite. So trees grow on other trees in Britain purely by accident. A seed may blow into a wet cavity or patch of rot in an older stem and find conditions suitable for growth. Alternatively a bird or small animal may carry a seed up an old tree trunk and then be disturbed or forget to eat it. Trees growing on other trees are called 'air' or 'cuckoo' trees. The advantage of living on another tree is the lack of competition from ground vegetation, but there are disadvantages. In a dry summer the moisture in an old stem might dry up. A winter gale may blow the whole tree down; this is very likely if the interloper is successful and gets too big and heavy for its precarious location.

A oakwood on the west coast of Scotland, where the warm, damp conditions are ideal for mosses, lichens and ferns.

What are lichens?

Lichens are organisms made up by the association of algae and fungi. The algal cells of the lichen use atmospheric carbon dioxide to produce organic carbon sugars (see photosynthesis page 18) and use rain water and mineral nutrients from the atmosphere.

Does lichen kill trees?

No. Lichens are not parasites; they do not consume the host plant nor poison it; they are simply using the tree as something to grow upon. Lichens are epiphytes (one plant growing upon another living plant). Because of their small size and slow growth, lichens thrive in places where higher plants have difficulty growing and can tolerate extended periods of severe desiccation and cold. This means that they can grow in habitats unsuitable for most other plants: bare rock, walls, roofs and the trunks and branches of trees. They also provide food for the larvae of a number of moths including the footman species (e.g. common and hoary) and marbled beauty.

Why do mosses and ferns grow on trees?

Mosses, ferns, liverworts and other plants growing on trees are called epiphytes. They are there because they have colonized a niche that meets their exact needs for growth. Usually their nutrient requirements are modest and they will only develop on trees that are growing where there is enough moisture. Many, particularly ferns, also need a degree of shade. Most epiphytes could not survive on the ground where competition from herbaceous plants would suppress them.

Does ivy kill trees?

Ivy is not parasitic – the root-like structures on the aerial shoots of ivy cannot absorb moisture and nutrients from the host tree and the aerial 'roots' do not penetrate into the wood of the host. Ivy roots in the soil may compete with those of the support tree for moisture and nutrients, but by the time the tree trunk is sturdy enough to become a support for ivy, its roots are likely to have extended well away from the base of the trunk which is where the ivy roots will initially colonize.

Once the shoots of the ivy extend into the crown of the tree, competition at the roots for water and nutrients may have some significance, particularly if the tree is old and in serious decline. The most adverse effect ivy can have on a tree arises when the adult/reproductive ivy shoots spread in a dense mass over the support tree's crown.

In the senile tree, the remaining crown may become swamped and the weight of the ivy can then cause a tree with rotting roots to topple over in a strong wind. Healthy trees are normally unaffected because their crowns allow insufficient light through for the ivy to grow strongly.

This black poplar, until recently, had ivy growing around the trunk. It has now been thinned by tree surgeons so that the crown will not become choked with ivy.

Despite the threats to sick trees, ivy has considerable conservation benefits, providing a habitat for small mammals like voles, and nesting opportunities for a wide range of birds, including the wren, song-thrush and spotted flycatcher. Ivy flowers also provide late nectar in autumn and early fruit in March and April, while cattle, sheep, deer and horses will browse ivy foliage in hard winter weather.

What is honey fungus?

It is a fungus with the Latin name *Armillaria mellea*. The visible parts are the fruit bodies that appear on the tree or near to it or the black 'bootlaces' or rhizomorphs that may be found under the bark, attached to roots or sometimes tracing their way through soil.

Is honey fungus a problem?

Honey fungus is not always a problem. There are at least four recognised species of *Armillaria*. These vary from weak parasites to aggressive parasites. The former appear to predominate in woodland, the latter can be a problem in gardens.

How can I get rid of, or protect my tree from, honey fungus?

If you think you have honey fungus check the diagnosis, since there are several types and not all of them are strongly pathogenic. *Phytophthora* or drought may be the culprit followed by a benign form of honey fungus. A few trees are resistant: for example, box, hornbeam, beech, ash, holly, larch and yew. There is no 'official' control therapy but a former head gardener at Stourhead, Wiltshire used to successfully hold back progress of the disease with Jeyes Fluid and a watering can.

The safest way to avoid honey fungus is not to plant a new tree where infected trees have been, which means keeping well away from the stumps and root spread of those trees. Most often the fungus spreads through contact with old diseased roots and buried wood in the ground. Although new outbreaks from fungal spores can occur where trees have basal damage, these are much less of a threat. There is little point in removing fructifications (toadstools) because spores travel miles and they are everywhere. Avoid staking young trees with untreated posts: they are a common source of new infection once they come into contact with wet soil.

Are all fungi bad for trees?

There are some 50,000 fungi species recorded but there may be up to 250,000 in existence. The saprophytic fungi feed by digesting dead organic material – an important function in the recycling of plant matter.

Above: A typical bracket fungus, many species of which occur on trees.

Opposite: Honey fungus can be a problem for weak or old trees.

The heartwood of a tree can be decomposed by some very specialist white, brown and soft rot fungi which decompose this wood. Hollowing is now seen as an entirely natural process – and is an exceptionally valuable and rare habitat. The fungi start the process of decay and the softened tissues are then eaten by a range of other organisms including some very specialist beetles. The breakdown products from this process are recycled through aerial roots or return to the soil to the advantage of the tree.

Generally speaking, so-called parasitic fungi (e.g. *phytophthoras*) become significant when a tree or part of a tree is under stress. At our current level of knowledge it appears that they can colonize and digest live tissue and eventually contribute to a tree's demise.

Trees and Wildlife

How can I tell if my tree has bats?

The tree must be large and probably quite old with dry holes, cavities or splits in it. These need not be very large, on the surface at least: the most common British bat, the pipistrelle, will fit inside a matchbox. In summer, larger cavities are required for females, which gather together in maternity colonies. The best proof of the presence of bats is to see them leaving the tree at dusk and even to hear squeaking from inside. Entrance holes often have dark staining around them with tiny scratch marks from claws. Droppings may be found which look like mouse droppings but they are composed of insect fragments, making them crumbly. Under the 1981 Wildlife and Countryside Act it is illegal to damage or obstruct a bat roost. Sightings should be reported to your local bat group.

Which British tree supports most insect life?

Research by Oxford University in conjunction with the Biological Records Centre at Monks Wood has resulted in published league tables for the numbers of different insect species living on the leaves of particular tree species throughout Britain. These suggest that willow supports the most, with 450 species, but these occur on five willow species. Oak supports 423 on two species, pedunculate and sessile. The top score for the number of different species on a single tree is hawthorn (*Crataegus monogyna*) with 209.

These data should not be regarded as the final word, since new finds on all species of tree are constantly being reported. A lot depends on the ecosystem: for example, a tree in mixed woodland is likely to support more insects than one in isolation. In some areas, however, atmospheric pollution is taking its toll of micro-organisms so numbers are severely reduced. Interestingly some exotic trees are finding favour with British insects: in Wales, for example, southern beech (*Nothofagus obliqua*) is home to many insects that are more usually found on oak.

Taking trees as a whole, rather than just those supporting leaf-eating insects, the picture is somewhat different. The wood

Birds such as the fieldfare depend on food sources like hawthorn berries throughout the winter.

decay insects and those associated with leaf litter, blossom and fruits and seeds are also important. Sycamore is extremely valuable for wildlife biomass because it supports a superabundance of aphids on which aphid feeders can feast.

Which trees are good for bees?

Many flowering trees are nectar producers, providing food for bees. Probably the most important are sallow willows (pussy willow) that flower very early in the year when little else is available for bees to forage. Most valuable in summer are limes, their sweet smell attracting thousands of bees on hot afternoons. Other spring flowering trees that attract bees are crab apple, cherry, sycamore and hawthorn. In summer, cotoneaster, holly, Indian bean,

whitebeam, eucryphia and the tulip tree are particularly useful. In the autumn, ivy flowers are essential food for the last bees of the year.

Which trees are good for birds?

All trees are good for birds, since they provide a mixture of shelter, safe perches, nesting sites and, in many cases, food. For perching birds, trees are essential to keep them out of reach of ground predators. Although some species, such as wrens, are most at home in 'native woodland', many birds will often be found amongst exotic trees in parks and gardens. So, when planting trees to attract birds, diversification should be the key (e.g. thorns in which to nest, and berry or fruit bearing species for food).

Tree
Pests

Are deer a problem for trees?

There are six deer species in the UK: red, roe, sika, fallow, muntjac and Chinese water deer. The populations of all but the Chinese water deer are increasing rapidly as there are no natural predators to control their expansion. Unfortunately deer browse young trees, damage saplings with their antlers and strip the bark from older trees and therefore can become a serious problem, especially in managed coppice or new woodland.

How can I stop deer eating my trees?

The Forestry Commission suggests that there are four main methods of controlling deer damage to trees:

1. Reduce deer numbers by shooting them and reducing the population to a level where the damage to the trees is

Deer and grey squirrels may seem very appealing, but they can cause great damage to trees – (above) small-leaved lime chewed by deer and (right) a fine young oak in the Forest of Dean ruined by squirrels.

not too severe (this cannot be done without a licence).

2. Physically protect trees from deer by using tree guards, fences or 'natural' protection such as 'dead hedging' – piling brash and old branches around the trees.

3. Reduce the significance of deer damage by, for example, increasing the density of young trees rather than by decreasing the rate of browsing.

4. Reduce the attractiveness of trees to deer by planting species that are less attractive to deer (e.g. alder or birch) or using the approved chemical repellent 'Aaprotect' (usually successful only in the short-term during the winter months).

Are grey squirrels a problem for trees?

Grey squirrels eat seeds, buds, flowers, shoots, nuts, berries and fruit from many trees and shrubs. They also eat fungi and insects, and occasionally birds' eggs and fledglings. The damage they can do to trees can be extensive, particularly where the sap is close to the surface of the tree, e.g. beech and sycamore. On the positive side, squirrels store nuts in the ground in the autumn, and do not always remember where they store them. They rely on scent to find the nuts but are not always very successful, so in effect they can help by 'planting' many tree seeds.

Ageing a tree

How do you find out the age of a tree?

The usual answer to this question is to count the rings, but this does not give the age of the tree – only the age of the stump at the height it was cut. It is possible to bore into a stem to count rings but this is not recommended and is not possible without specialist equipment.

In 1994 the Forestry Commission (FC) published a method of estimating the age of large and veteran trees. This relies on comparisons with a considerable amount of historical data, detailed observation of site types and understanding patterns of growth. There is no easy 'rule of thumb' that can be applied to estimating tree age; tree growth rates are far too complex and sensitive to environmental changes. The FC method is based initially on girth measurements and the use of tables; a calculator is essential for the mathematics. You can get copies of this information from the Forestry Commission by writing to *FC Publications, PO Box 25, Wetherby, West Yorkshire LS23 7EW*, and asking for the free paper on ageing trees by John White.

An alternative way of calculating age is to delve into the history of a particular site. Old maps and records may give an idea of when particular trees first appeared.

How do you estimate the height of a tree?

A makeshift way of measuring height is to find a stick, bracken stem or straw that can be cut off or folded back to the exact distance from your eye (measure with extreme care) to a grasping finger and thumb with the arm at full stretch. This stick is personal to you and will not work for anybody else. The stick should then be held out straight in front of you in a vertical position. The tree is aligned behind it and you move backwards or forwards until the tip of the tree appears to be at the top of the stick and the base appears to be at the bottom. The distance from your feet to the tree is now equal to the height of the tree.

To get an accurate girth, reflecting the age of this veteran oak, the measurement has been taken just below the heavy burring.

How do you measure the girth of a tree?

Measuring girth when no tape measure is at hand can best be done with string, a dog lead or a non-stretchy item of clothing. Short lengths can be measured repeatedly around the stem and counted up until you arrive back at the starting point. The height recommended by the Tree Register of the British Isles (TROBI) at which trees should be measured is called 'breast height' – 1.5 metres (5 feet) above ground level. Measurement is not always easy as there can be lumps and bumps around the stem (particularly if the tree is old). The measurement should then best be taken to avoid any obvious burrs (see page 37). In any event, remember to record the height above the ground where the measurement was taken. The national records held by

TROBI uses 'Diameter at Breast Height', so divide the measured girth by pi (π) (3.14159) to obtain this dimension.

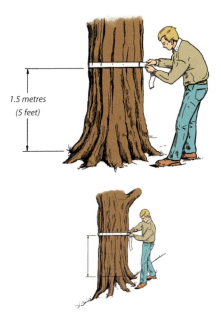

1.5 metres
(5 feet)

Apple Trees

How many apple varieties are there in Britain?

Approximately 20,000 named apple varieties have existed worldwide with approximately 2,500 varieties being grown in Britain since Roman times, of which some 780 are native. Of these c2,300 varieties are growing at the National Apple Collection at Brogdale in Kent, but many old varieties have become extinct or are growing unrecorded elsewhere in Britain.

How can I graft an apple tree?

There are many different methods of grafting. However, the basic principle is to join the graft material or scion from one tree – a shoot – with the rootstock from another (usually of the same species) to make a new tree. Both are cut and the two cut surfaces are bound together until they fuse and become one. The resulting tree will then grow with some of the characteristics of its rootstock.

How do you identify unknown apples?

This is difficult to answer as there are so many types and forms of apples. Excellent reference books on apples include *Apples* by John Bultitude, Macmillan ISBN 0 333 34971 7, 1984

(out of print and probably expensive second-hand); *The English Apple* by Rosanne Sanders, Phaidon ISBN 0 7148 2498 9, 1988; and *The New Book of Apples* by Joan Morgan and Alison Richards, Ebury Press ISBN 0 09 1883 98 9, revised in 2003.

Apples can be sent to the National Apple Collection at Brogdale for identification. Three samples of typical mature fruit should be sent, plus a sample shoot and leaves, and as much detail about the fruit and tree as possible: its season of use, whether it is a dessert or culinary apple, the age and habit of the tree, and its location if different from your address. Samples sent for identification should be clearly labeled and carefully packed together with (in block capitals) your name, Friends of Brogdale membership number (if applicable), address, postcode and phone number, plus the appropriate fee (see below) and a stamped, addressed envelope for the reply. If more than one cultivar is sent, number the fruits and keep a record, as samples cannot be returned. Apples are best numbered on the skin with a ballpoint or waterproof marker pen. To ensure that the fruit arrives in good condition, wrap in newspaper or bubble wrap in a box and post first class to: *Fruit Identification, Brogdale Horticultural Trust, Brogdale Road, Faversham, Kent ME13 8XZ.* A fee will be payable, please contact Brogdale for details. Please be patient as many apples can be received at the same time, and it may take some time to respond to your questions.

A tiny selection of apples grown in Britain showing the remarkable diversity of colour and form. From left to right: Bramley's Seedling, Adam's Pearmain, Keswick Codling, Court Pendu Plat, Egremont Russet and Dabinett.

Typical view of a modern, productive apple orchard in Britain, but Dr Juniper (inset) on his travels to Tian Shan discovers where the progenitors of these apples still grow today in dense mountain forests.

Where did apples originate?

For many years, there was a debate about whether apples (*Malus domestica*) evolved from chance hybridisation among various wild species. Recent research by Dr Barrie Juniper of Oxford University and others, has indicated, however, that the hybridisation theory is probably false. Instead, it appears that a single species still growing in the Tian Shan in China and Kazakhstan is the progenitor of the apples we eat today.

Leaves taken from trees in this area showed them all to belong to the species *Malus pumila* (previously known as *M. sieversii*), with some genetic sequences common to *M. domestica*.

Dr Juniper suggests that in the high valleys of Tian Shan, mammals, particularly bears, wild pigs and horses, selected the larger sweeter fruits very similar to those we know today. Much later humans began to penetrate this area and domesticated the horse with its developed taste for the apple. Trade facilitated the spread of the fruit along the 'Silk Roads' that extended from China towards the Middle East and into Western Europe.

What are the different apple rootstocks (M series)?

Developed at the Malling Institute in Kent, the Malling-Merton series of standard rootstocks for apples enables the tree grower to manipulate the tree's eventual size. Apple tree rootstocks are referred to by numbers prefixed by letters, indicating the developer of the rootstock. The most often used rootstocks are:

M27: Extremely dwarfing: produces a tree 2 metres (6 feet) high.

M9: Very dwarfing: reaches a height of 3 metres (8 to 10 feet).

M26: Dwarfing: more vigorous and generally stronger than M9, with a height of 2.5 to 3 metres (8 to 10 feet).

MM106: Semi-dwarfing: produces a tree with an eventual height of 4 to 5.5 metres (14 to 18 feet).

M111: Vigorous – not generally suitable for gardens, being both too large and spreading – eventual height 5.5 to 8 metres (18 to 25 feet).

M25: Very vigorous – suitable for a grassed orchard, and trees can grow to a height of 4.5 to 6 metres (15 to 20 feet).

Where the name begins with an M, the rootstock was developed at Merton in London. MM means it was developed at Malling Merton (Malling being in Kent). MM rootstocks are more resistant to woolly aphids.

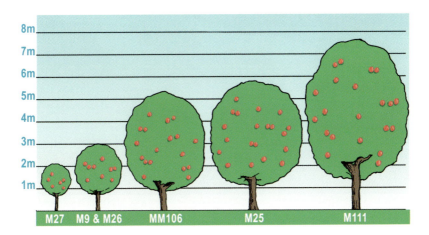

Trees and Weather

Are trees dangerous if they bend in the wind?

Research has shown that young stems need to flex in order to build up thickness and strength. This is partly why it is preferable to give a newly-planted tree a short stake rather than a long one that will hold the tree rigidly. While trees bend they are safe, but when the wind becomes so strong that they are unable to dissipate its energy by bending away from it, damage starts to occur: broken branches, broken stems or even uprooting may occur.

Below: The incredible effect of regular high winds on Scots pines on the east coast of Scotland.

What impact will climatic change have on trees?

Familiar species may not survive where they are now but trees in general look set to take every advantage of climate change. Although the pace of physical change to the biosphere is accelerating, driven by polluting (greenhouse) gases resulting directly or indirectly from human activity, for trees this may not be destructive. Many trees that have evolved within a particular climate range will have to adapt, migrate or perish. It is thought that some conifers will thrive closer to the polar regions but die out in some of their existing strongholds, e.g. the Atlas Mountains. Trees adapted to hot conditions are likely to colonize temperate areas. Already, for example, eucalyptus species survive in places, where they would have been damaged by frost only 25 years ago. Our biggest worry may be the pests and pathogens that benefit from climate change which may cause damage to trees in the future.

Should I shelter under trees in a thunderstorm?

Emphatically no. Although oaks and redwoods are the trees most likely to be severely damaged by lightning, no tree is safe. When caught in a storm in open countryside the safest thing to do is to sit or crouch on something dry or made of rubber under a hedge, on a large straw bale or in a barn. This is better than pressing on into open spaces. Keep away from wire fences and overhead power lines. When in town, seek shelter in a building or a vehicle. Do not use an umbrella or hold on to metal objects.

Is it true that a decaying tree gives off methane?

Yes, it is true that the organisms 'decaying' a dead tree give off methane. It is an organic compound that is being recycled into the atmosphere as a gas. All decaying vegetation produces this colourless, odourless but highly volatile combination of carbon and hydrogen. It is the main part of natural gas: in fenland it is known as marsh gas and in coal mines as firedamp. Along with carbon dioxide, methane is one of the so-called greenhouse gases. However decaying trees only return to the atmosphere what they have taken out of it during their lifetime so a balanced cycle is maintained: their contribution has nothing to do with methane liberated from a fossilised organism.

Left: An ancient olive grove in Spain. A recent commercial planting of olive trees in Devon may signal future trends in Britain due to climate change.

Which trees are most likely to suffer/benefit from droughts in Britain?

Most drought damage to established trees is not caused directly by lack of rainfall but by human activities that aggravate the situation: for example, water abstraction that can lower water tables. Damage, or death, are more a matter of artificial conditions than sensitive tree species. However, amalanchier, pear, alder, beech, spruce, fir and sweet gum do appear to be vulnerable to drought. Trees that benefit from dry conditions include eucalyptus, tree of heaven, sweet chestnut, aspen, grey poplar and false acacia.

Can trees reduce flooding?

Yes, in several ways. Initially trees in forests intercept a proportion of rainfall so that it never reaches the ground. When it dries, wet foliage returns water as vapour to the atmosphere. Trees also take water away from the soil so it is able to absorb more when flood conditions occur. Tree roots bind soil together, helping to reduce run-off; the primary cause of flash flooding. Belts of fibrous rooted trees (e.g. *Salix cinerea*, the grey sallow) close to watercourses will absorb the force of rising flood water and eventually trap flotsam until an absorbent bank builds up between the trees.

Which trees are good for producing shade?

All trees produce shade. In many circumstances, especially with a changing climate, shade may become an increasingly desirable commodity, especially for houses or conservatories where it may be necessary to reduce the effect of hot summers.

Deciduous shade trees include the horse chestnut, but this is a brittle, unsafe tree in old age. A better choice is the Indian horse chestnut (*Aesculus indica*) which flowers profusely in late June and saves its conkers until November. Italian alder (*Alnus cordata*) casts a pleasant shade and does not demand a wet site. The ubiquitous town shade tree is London plane but its ultimate height of 35 metres (115 feet), a crown spread of more than 20 metres (66 feet) and a stem diameter of over 1 metre (over 3 feet), rule it out for all but the widest city streets.

In the right conditions some conifers or even palms may be appropriate. Climatic change in Britain means that previously tender trees such as holm oak (*Quercus ilex*) and cork oak (*Quercus suber*) will thrive in most cities in the British Isles. Harder to find, but worth the search, is Turner's oak (*Quercus* × *turneri*) which looks just like a common oak but retains its leaves all winter.

*Two useful choices of shade trees – the holm oak
(above) and the London plane (below).*

Good trees for producing shade:
Mirbeck oak (*Quercus canariensis*)
Beech (*Fagus sylvatica*)
Cedar (*Cedrus* species)
Foxglove tree (*Paulownia fargesii*)
Holm oak (*Quercus ilex*)
Horse chestnut
(*Aesculus hippocastanum*)
Indian bean tree (*Catalpa bignonioides*)
London plane (*Platanus* × *hispanica*)
Lucombe oak
(*Quercus* × *hispanica* 'Lucombeana')
Norway maple (*Acer platanoides*)
Tulip tree (*Liriodendron tulipifera*)

Tree Planting

Why thin trees after planting?

Young trees benefit from close proximity to one another where they are protected from environmental extremes, especially gales, drying out and competition from ground vegetation. In a commercial plantation all the trees come up together and form straight stems. In urban planting they grow into recognisable trees instead of rather haphazard bushes. Thinning is needed when the trees themselves start to compete for light.

Good management, with the objective of producing valuable timber or fine looking trees, will require thinning several times until only the best trees remain. Thinning enables the forester or arborist to manipulate mixtures, gradually removing 'nurse' species, broken or badly forked stems or individuals that have not grown very

well. The life expectancy of a tree is such that planting only one is a huge risk – it is better to plant five and gradually take out the four that get damaged or diseased.

Why not plant bigger trees?

Taking a tree from a nursery and planting it out in the open is a traumatic experience for the tree: it is coming from a sheltered environment and going into isolation and exposure. Heavy standard trees require substantial support to alleviate this. Young bare rooted trees always suffer some root damage in transplanting. This upsets the root to shoot balance. Die-back will result until the top of the tree is reduced to a size that is sustainable by the roots. None of these problems is so bad if small plants are used. Generally, small newly planted trees will overtake large ones in just a few years. Even if the root system remains intact (in some form of container) problems remain, and the root will take a long time to extend into the adjacent soil. During this time the tree might roll around and finish up leaning.

Are there grants for tree planting?

Yes, there are a number of grants for tree planting. Small grants for schools and community plantings are available from many organisations including The Tree Council, and large scale grants for woodland planting are available from the Forestry Commission. Grant schemes can, however, change year on year, and keeping track of what is available is sometimes difficult. The Royal Forestry Society has therefore pulled together much of the information on grants and this can be obtained from the Society's website on **www.rfs.org.uk/grantsfortrees.asp**

What questions should be asked before tree planting?

When choosing a tree it is essential to think about the roles the tree will serve. Many objectives can be met at once – good autumn colour, a pleasing shape, shade and wildlife benefits are all possible from a single well chosen tree. The ideal is to plant a tree that can grow to full maturity with little or no tree surgery. Mistakes in planting a tree are long lasting, expensive and difficult to rectify.

Successful tree planting depends upon good decisions in relation to the tree and to the site. It is easy to cut down a 'wrong' tree but it is very difficult to establish a different one in its place if it was part of a planting scheme. Vision and faith are needed from the very start because a sapling that can be held between two fingers could eventually become huge and live for hundreds of years.

Two young tree planters at a planting, grant-aided by The Tree Council.

What is meant by the provenance of trees?

'Provenance' simply means where the seed of the plant originated. It does not refer to the origin of the species, although this may also be the case. In forestry, provenances of Monterey pine (*Pinus radiata*), for example, include California and Baja California in Mexico as well as Britain and other countries where second generation seed is collected. Therefore a tree of local provenance is one whose seed is collected close to the place to be planted. This does not however mean that the parent tree is native to the area where its seed was collected, if the parent was an introduced tree!

Tree monocultures – good or bad?

Single species plantations are prone to disease or insect predation that can rapidly spread unchecked. Conifer monocultures are also at serious risk of forest fire. Diversity is an insurance against unknown health or damage risks and it also provides a lifeline for wildlife in and under the trees. Monocultures are only sustainable with considerable levels of management and manipulation.

I've heard of genetically modified trees – what are they?

One thrust of genetic research in forestry for the past 50 years has been towards tree breeding using selected parents of high quality. This is usually done by establishing orchards of 'mother trees' pollinated with material collected from 'plus' trees from elsewhere. Productive hybrids such as hybrid larch have also been deliberately produced in the same way. In horticulture, genetic modification is more sophisticated and likely to be used increasingly on trees intended to produce fruit, non-wood products (e.g. rubber or medicines) or ornamental perfection.

Hybrid poplars, all of the same Serotena clone, growing in a plantation. If disease strikes one of these trees it is quite likely that all the others will become infected, as they are all genetically identical.

Tree Diseases

What are the first signs of sudden oak death?

Sudden oak death is an infection of a tree by a fungus called *Phytophthora ramorum*, a species related to the fungus that caused the Irish potato famine. The name 'Sudden Oak Death' (SOD) is something of a misnomer because it also affects beech, sweet and horse chestnut and holm oak, along with Douglas fir and Sitka spruce, as well as some shrubs including rhododendron and viburnum. In addition there have been findings on pieris, camellia, syringa, kalmia and single findings on pot-grown yew and witch hazel plants.

An early symptom of an infected tree may be a sudden deterioration in foliage colour. Further examination is needed. The trunks of infected trees develop cankers that have brown to black discoloured outer bark on the lower trunk. These cankers seep dark red to black sap and are known as 'bleeding cankers' or 'tarry spots'. Removal of the bark reveals areas of mottled, necrotic, dead and discoloured inner bark tissue which may include black zone lines around the edges of necrotic tissues. Sudden death occurs when the cankers encircle stems, cutting off the water supply to foliage.

What are the first signs of Dutch elm disease?

The symptoms of Dutch elm disease (DED) are caused by a fungus infecting the water conducting system of the tree. The fungus causes clogging of vascular tissues, preventing water movement to the crown and causing visual symptoms as the leaves wilt and die.

Symptoms of DED begin as wilting of leaves, proceeding to yellowing and browning. Symptoms start to show in late spring or any time later during the growing season and may progress throughout the whole tree in a single season. Branches and stems of elms infected by the DED fungus typically develop dark streaks of discoloration. To detect discoloration, cut through and peel off the bark of a dying branch to expose the surface of the wood. In newly infected branches, brown streaks characteristically appear in the sapwood of the current year.

Typical manifestation of Dutch elm disease in a hedge and, below, an English elm in good shape near Brighton.

Another diagnostic characteristic of infected trees is that the terminal leaf on a branch remains withered but intact during the winter.

If there are healthy elm trees in hedges, will they die?

Elm trees in hedges will grow until they reach a size suitable for colonization by the two species of elm bark beetle (*Scolytus* species). It usually takes 20 to 30 years for the trees to reach the right size for colonization, if there are any beetles in the neighbourhood to carry the disease around. The result will be the death of the growing trees, but in English elm the root system will usually remain intact, allowing the trees to re-grow again from suckers in time.

Tree Care

My garden tree is too big – should I fell it?

Sometimes trees have to be removed before they are becoming a hazard. If this seems likely it is best to take action quickly. Each year of delay the cost of removal will be spiralling and the hazard will be greater. Some trees can be given a new lease of life by pruning. Good pruning may extend the useful life of a tree but poor pruning can shorten it. If the tree does have to be felled, try to have the stump removed too, since decaying roots can be a source of disease and take a lot of nitrogen out of the soil.

Before commencing work, however, you need to be sure that your tree is not protected with a Tree Preservation Order or that you don't live in a Conservation Area (see page 98). Tree work can be dangerous and it is always best to seek professional help from a qualified tree surgeon before commencing any major tree work (see page 101).

When should I prune my trees?

The best answer to this is to observe nature. High winds, snow and ice storms help to keep trees safe by breaking off dead wood and weak branches on some species of tree, sometimes even removing the whole top of the tree. Most often this occurs in the autumn when there is still a weight of deciduous foliage, or in early winter in severe storms. So this is the best time to do most pruning. Do not delay until late winter because by then sap will be rising. There are particular types of pruning that must be done at other times of year to promote fruit or flowers or reduce the incidence of disease but in general following nature's example is best. It is generally accepted that any significant pruning is not done after long periods of drought or long periods of cold frosty weather.

Left: This ancient yew tree in Wiltshire has been full of concrete for over a hundred years. However this is not a recommended procedure today.

Opposite: When this monkey puzzle was first planted about a hundred years ago, nobody seems to have considered how big it might actually become.

How do I stop a tree being vandalised?

It is not possible to stop mindless vandalism by determined perpetrators. Education of some form is extremely valuable (this may be at least some information signs) but best of all is to involve potential vandals in the planting scheme ('poacher' to become 'gamekeeper'). Another important aspect of urban planting schemes is to keep the site tidy and looking cared for: a derelict site simply cries out for misdemeanours to be perpetrated. Another piece of good psychology is not to glorify vandalism (in the vandal's eyes) by giving it publicity. If all this fails there are 'vandal proof' trees such as Syrian juniper, black locust and monkey puzzle that have vicious thorns.

Alternatively aspen, hybrid wingnut and false acacia (again) which sucker freely when chopped down. Be wary of these, however, as they can become invasive

Should a hollow tree be filled with concrete?

In the past it was thought that hollow trees should always be filled up with something. Concrete was a favourite but bricks, tar and stones have also been used. We now know that the last thing you should do with a hollow tree is fill it with anything. Cement and live or dead wood do not adhere to one another, so very soon after completing the job the join fails and water gets in. This accelerates rot and provides a haven for wood-decaying organisms.

Tree Preservation Orders

What is a Tree Preservation Order (TPO)?

It is an order made by a local planning authority (London boroughs, district or unitary councils and occasionally county councils and national parks authorities) which in general makes it an offence to cut down, top, lop, uproot, wilfully damage or wilfully destroy a tree without the planning authority's permission.

What types of trees can be covered by a TPO?

All types, including hedge trees, but not hedges, bushes or shrubs. The order can cover anything from a single tree to entire woodlands.

What are the penalties for working on a protected tree without permission?

If a protected tree is deliberately destroyed, or damaged in a manner likely to destroy it, there are fines of up to £20,000 if convicted in the magistrates' court. In determining the amount of the fine, the court will take account of any financial benefit arising from the offence.

For other offences the fines are up to £2,500. Normally a replacement tree will be required if the tree was cut down or destroyed.

Are all oak trees protected?

Although it appears to be a widely held belief, it is not true that all oak trees are protected by law. Some oak trees are protected by specific TPOs but, as a whole class, oaks throughout Britain are not protected.

My house is in a 'Conservation Area'. Are there any extra restrictions on trees in a Conservation Area?

Yes. The local planning authority needs to be given six weeks' notice before any work is carried out on trees which are located in a Conservation Area but are not yet the subject of a TPO. This gives the authority an opportunity to consider whether an order should be made to protect the trees.

Permission is not needed if work is to be undertaken on trees less than 7.5 centimetres (3 inches) in diameter,

The Comiston House Corsican pine, in the suburbs of Edinburgh, is one of Scotland's noted heritage trees and is protected by a TPO.

measured 1.5 metres (5 feet) above the ground, or 10 centimetres (4 inches in diameter) if thinning to help the growth of other trees. If in any doubt, check with the local planning authority.

For more questions and answers on Tree Preservation Orders – see the leaflet produced by Communities and Local Government called *Protected Trees: A Guide to Tree Preservation Procedures*, which can be downloaded from their website at:

**www.communities.gov.uk/
treesandhedges**

Tree People

What is a Tree Warden?

A Tree Warden is a volunteer who champions his or her local trees. The Tree Council's Tree Warden Scheme is a national force of local volunteers dedicated to their community's trees in town, city and countryside across the UK. It gives people who feel that trees matter an opportunity to:

- champion their local trees and woods
- play an active role in protecting and improving the treescape
- involve their neighbours in tree projects
- get together with like-minded people for training and field trips
- carry out a range of practical activities.

The Tree Council, which launched the Tree Warden Scheme in 1990, co-ordinates it nationally and works with local authorities, voluntary organisations, parish councils and local partnerships to set up and develop Tree Warden networks.

Today there are many thousands of Tree Wardens in local networks throughout the UK, forming a volunteer force of immense value for the environment. Together they devote nearly two million hours a year (worth about £13 million) to voluntary tree-related activities.

These volunteers work closely with local authority officers and conservation bodies, who are key to the scheme's success. Activities include:

- planting and caring for trees
- woodland management
- setting up tree nurseries using seeds collected locally
- surveying trees and gathering information about them
- providing early warning of threats, disease, decay, or vandalism
- spearheading Tree Council initiatives, such as its Hedge Tree Campaign to reverse the decline of trees in hedges.

As local tree champions, Tree Wardens are the eyes and ears of their neighbourhoods. Community involvement is a central aim of the scheme. Some Tree Wardens work with local schools or groups, developing imaginative projects to encourage others to value the community's trees and woods.

What is a tree officer?

A 'tree officer' is an officer of the local planning authority responsible for Tree Preservation Orders and trees in Conservation Areas (see page 98) plus other duties concerning trees in the authority area.

Tree surgeon at work

How can I find a good tree surgeon?

Competent tree surgeons will have certificates which show they have been trained or assessed. They may have academic qualifications in arboriculture and will use safety equipment to protect you, your property and themselves. The Arboriculture Association's recommendation for choosing a good tree surgeons is to ask for a quote – the reputable arborist will offer a written quote; will work to British Standard BS3998; will be insured and will provide a phone number or contact details for a previous client. The quote should also contain full details of the work to be undertaken, which will explain what will happen to the debris, whether VAT is included, who will be responsible for obtaining legal permissions (if required) and the steps that will be taken to protect you and your property.

In the UK there are also two schemes certifying the competence of arborists and you should ask if the tree surgeon is an Arboricultural Association approved contractor or an International Society of Arboriculture Certified Arborist. Membership of one of these Schemes provides a level of competence in the contractor that should help you in your choice.

What is a 'tree hugger'?

The Chipko movement was a group of villagers in the Uttarakhand region of India who opposed commercial logging. The demonstration took place spontaneously in April 1973 in the village of Mandal in the upper Alakananda valley. The movement was best known for its tactic of hugging trees to prevent them being cut down. This gave rise to the term 'tree hugger' as a slang term for environmentalists.

Celebrating trees

How can I make sloe gin?

Pick your sloes from blackthorn hedges in October or November when they are ripest – probably after the first frosts. Take half a litre of gin in a litre bottle, cut or prick the sloes and drop them into the half-empty bottle so that they displace the gin to near the top. Add 150 grams (5.25 ounces) of sugar, seal the bottle and then turn or agitate the bottle daily for a week, then weekly for a month or two. Although it will then be ready to drink, it is really best kept until the next winter.

Where did the game of conkers come from and why are they called conkers?

The first recorded game of conkers using horse chestnuts was on the Isle of Wight in 1848. Until then, children used snail shells or hazelnuts. The word conker is derived from a 19th century dialect word for a snail shell. In 1965 the World Conker Championships were set up on the village green at Ashton (near Oundle), Northamptonshire, and still take place on the second Sunday of October each year.

Who invented Christmas trees?

In the 7th century a monk from Crediton, Devonshire – St Boniface – went to Germany to teach about God. Legend has it that he used the triangular shape of the fir tree to describe the Holy Trinity. People thus began to revere the fir tree instead of the oak. In 1601 a visitor to Strasbourg, Germany, recorded trees decorated with "wafers and golden sugar-twists (barleysugar) and paper flowers of all colours" at a Christmas market. Christmas trees came to Britain with the German Georgian Kings in the 17th century, but did not become fashionable with the British public until Queen Victoria and her German Prince, Albert, were featured in the *Illustrated London News* in 1846. Once Victoria took up the idea, Christmas trees (Norway spruce) became popular with the public and the rest is history.

Which is the world's tallest known Christmas tree?

The world's tallest cut Christmas tree was a Douglas fir 67 metres (220 feet) high, erected and decorated at Northgate Shopping Center, Seattle, Washington, USA, in December 1950.

One of the recent winners of the World Conker Championships and (right) the huge Christmas tree erected every year in Trafalgar Square.

Which Christmas trees don't drop their needles?

The traditional cut Norway spruce Christmas tree has a habit of dropping its needles before the end of Christmas. Although it is the traditional tree, its popularity has waned recently in favour of species which will retain their needles longer. These included Nordman fir (with good needle retaining properties and soft, wide and flat, dark green needles); Fraser fir (similar to the Nordman fir in its needle retaining properties but narrower crown, making it an ideal Christmas tree if space is at a premium); Douglas fir (with long citrus smelling needles which are retained well) and Scots pine (an excellent needle retaining tree which scents a room with pine smells).

Curiosities

What is the substance that drips from lime trees?

The substance that drips like fine rain in summer from smooth-leaved lime species is honeydew. It is excreted by sap-sucking insects such as aphids and scale insects. Ants 'farm' the aphids to supplement their diet, by collecting the honeydew from them like milk from a cow. Black mould rapidly invades the sticky coated leaves and stems. It is unsightly but harmless.

Why do willows take root from cuttings?

Willows are pioneer trees so many, but not all, root from cuttings. Wetland species have adapted to dropping twigs and small branches into rivers where they take root in wet mud. The crack willow has particularly weak shoots making it adept at this: so good in fact that whole single sex populations have developed which do not produce viable seed and rely entirely on vegetative propagation.

Why do some trees grow taller in woodlands than in the open?

In order to survive, trees rely on green foliage. This can only develop in full light. In dense woodlands, trees have to grow upwards to reach the light, becoming ever taller in the process. Even so the crown (the branches and leaves) will still be limited in size because of competition from adjacent trees. This is not detrimental because root systems are similarly restrained and the whole tree remains in balance. Trees in the open conform to the same root to shoot ratio principle, so when the crown of an open grown tree is in balance with the root it has no further need to expand – certainly not upwards where exposure to wind becomes a problem in isolated situations.

Which familiar trees are poisonous?

All tree foliage should be regarded as unsuitable for human consumption and even fruit should be treated with respect (for example, it is said that one hundred almonds eaten in one go could kill!). The most toxic common trees in the British Isles are laburnum, yew, buckthorn, privet, daphne species, laurel and spindle. Others such as juniper species, red cedar, cotoneaster, ivy and many more can cause irritant rashes, internal inflammation, vomiting or hyperactivity.

Above: Regenerating limes in dense woodland grow tall and straight as they seek the sunlight.
Left: The beautiful, but poisonous laburnum.

Ancient trees

What is an ancient tree?

The term 'ancient tree' is one that is not capable of precise definition but it encompasses trees of three categories:

- trees of interest biologically, aesthetically or culturally because of their age
- trees in the last stage of their life
- trees that are old relative to others of the same species

A tree in the last phase of its life that has retrenched can be very healthy and vigorous despite extensive decay and dieback.

What is a veteran tree?

The term is used to describe the wildlife or habitat quality of trees which are not yet ancient and focuses on a range of features associated with wood decay habitats in bark, root, trunk and branches. These habitat features, which are naturally found in the ancient stage, are 'prematurely' present at an earlier (pre-ancient) stage. Only trees showing significant wood decay habitats (veteran features) are recognised as veteran trees.

What is an ancient woodland?

'Ancient woodland' is a term that was coined during the 1980s in the UK, to refer to woodland dating back to at least 1600 in England and Wales (or 1750 in Scotland). These are the dates of the first detailed maps and before then the planting of new woodland was uncommon. Therefore a woodland present in 1600 is likely to have developed naturally and to have been woodland for possibly many hundreds if not thousands of years. However, few if any woodlands in the country have always been woodland, for it is thought that all areas of the country have been cleared by man at some point since we arrived on these islands.

What is a Green Monument?

The Tree Council's *Green Monuments Campaign* is a concerted effort by the UK's lead tree campaigning partnership to gain special protected status for trees of great historical, cultural or ecological significance – heritage trees.

The Tree Council has brought together its member organisations to campaign for:

- safeguards for green monuments
- encouragement for custodians to look after them
- support and advice on their care

The value of trees of historical, cultural or ecological importance is already formally recognised in many countries.

This is not the case in the UK. In contrast to historic buildings, there are no legal safeguards specific to ancient trees or others of heritage significance. Many of them could be felled tomorrow without penalty. Such protection that does exist for historic trees is coincidental and not by design.

The members of The Tree Council believe that such ancient and important trees should qualify as a form of historic monument and should be specifically protected.

Is a hollow tree dangerous?

Usually not. Recent exceptional storms have shown that hollow trees are blown down less frequently than solid ones. A cylinder is a stronger structure than a solid rod when exposed to a sideways force and the tree has far less weight on its roots. Ancient trees with reduced top branches and well buttressed stems are virtually permanent.

A remarkable and relatively unknown veteran oak in Yorkshire, the Laund Oak is right next to a road and could be said to be a vulnerable Green Monument.

This massive dead oak tree has been left standing in Windsor Great Park for its excellent habitat potential.

Is it good to leave dead trees standing?

From the point of view of the environment, yes. Standing dead trees are home and feeding station for many animals and birds and numerous insects. Some of the great historic landscape designers such as Humphry Repton recognised the importance of trees with decay and William Kent was known to import dead trees to create an immediate 'air of antiquity' to his landscape gardens. From a health and safety perspective leaving a dead tree standing may not be a good idea. Much depends upon the situation and amount of public access. A compromise may be to leave a safe stump and a pile of dead wood on the ground. A totally dead tree is unlikely to spread disease to live trees unless the adjacent trees are under stress already from some other cause.

What are stag-headed trees? Are they dying?

Stag-headed trees can be produced in one of two ways:

1. When a tree becomes old (for its species) it may begin to cut off the food supply to various branches – known as retrenching or 'growing downwards': as branches fall off naturally, the area of leaves available is reduced, resulting in the tree not producing enough new wood each year to cover it completely. The tree therefore 'cuts off' water and nutrients to certain branches which die, giving the characteristic 'stag-headed' form. This does not mean that the whole tree is about to die: it is a condition that can persist for many decades or even centuries.

2. Stag-heading can also occur in younger trees through drought, disease, insect damage, root disturbance, sunburn (in beech) or pollution. The response of the tree to the problem results in a new balance between the roots and the area of woody material and leaves; therefore some branches may die, creating the same 'stag-headed' appearance.

Typical appearance of a stag-headed oak in a medieval deer park.

Index